LeSS Case Study — Large Server Hardware Company

James Carpenter

Audio versions of this case study are *available here*

Synopsis

I strongly believe the best chance of long-term success is achieved with a broad product boundary coupled with feature teams executing within the full scope of the product. If the art of the possible excludes this choice, an incremental approach starting with *extended* (more cross-functional) component teams and aggressively moving towards *expanded* (more cross-component) component teams and feature teams can still be worth pursuing.

Benefits of this strategy within Nakashima's Modular Compute System division included:

- Locally improved **adaptability** and **value delivery** within the extended component boundary
- Improved technical practices that created **improved quality**, along with improved awareness of what additional improvements could bring
- Early identification and resolution of **defects** related to the extended component
- Improved employee **collaboration, engagement, and learning** within the extended component teams
- Increased awareness of **organizational impediments** and the need to make even more organizational changes

I hope you will find our success inspirational and instructive. Similarly, I hope you will avoid repeating our mistakes and instead spend your energy learning as you make new ones.

Skimming Hints

The case study is extremely long and detailed. If you prefer to skim it very quickly I recommend reading just the following:

- Synopsis section
- All figures and associated captions
- Conclusion section

Table of Contents

Overall Context of LeSS Adoption

Product Overview and People Involved

Nakashima's Modular Compute System (MCS) division is focused on product development for a family of integrated hardware, software, and networking components which collectively act as a complete pre-bundled in-house data center solution. It is to some extent an on-site forklift deployment of an Amazon Web Services type platform. Typical end customers are large banks, insurance companies, mobile phone providers, and scientific research organizations.

To help provide a sense of scale, the MCS division of Nakashima alone has somewhere on the order of a few thousand people. Most of the division's staff are concentrated in the greater metropolitan areas of San Francisco, Portland, and Bengaluru.

The entirety of the MCS division is focused on product development of the MCS product. All manufacturing including circuit board fabrication, metal fabrication, assembly, and other mass-production efforts are outsourced using specifications the MCS division creates.

Field support is handled by yet another division of Nakashima. The field support division focuses on providing a seamless customer support experience across all of Nakashima's products. Products supported by the field support division include a broad array of networking products such as telephone systems, video conferencing solutions, wireless networking solutions, and a host of other products that have nothing to do with MCS.

In practice, there are specialists within the field support division focused on supporting the MCS product. These specialists are exceptionally well positioned to observe the on-the-ground customer reality, and how it varies across the large and diverse MCS customer base. Due to the position of the field support specialists, engineers developing the MCS product can obtain some of the most useful and unfiltered feedback available by directly collaborating with these field support specialists.

The MCS product support staff and organizational capabilities should not be confused with what you might encounter for a typical mass consumer product. Rather this is the sort of quick responding, large budget technical support that comes with actual humans on-site when the need arises. Many of the field support specialists are just as knowledgeable and well-compensated in their area of expertise as are the engineers who develop the MCS product.

Trent Gambale was running the project management group within the MCS division, which consisted of less than a dozen project managers who helped coordinate the overall MCS development efforts. Much of the day to day project management facets were being handled by the various engineering directors within the MCS division. My initial sponsorship within the MCS division came through Trent, with active involvement of his VP and the Senior VP/GM at the time. Trent had heard of me through my previous work in another division within Nakashima.

Initial Agile Adoption Focus

The initial focus of the engagement was to assess a small handful of pre-existing (ostensibly) 'agile' teams, assist them in whatever improvements made sense, and to begin an agile adoption in other promising areas of the division we could identify.

After a few days of investigation, it became very clear all of the pre-existing 'agile' efforts were not. For example,

- Management routinely treated estimates as *commitments.*
- There was a lack of skillful engineering practices such as automated unit testing.
- There were no formal "inspect and adapt" events such as a retrospective.
- Teams were far from self-managing.

Following my initial examination of the pre-existing so-called agile efforts I discussed what I had learned with Trent. We judged the most effective place to focus our energy would be on creating new proper cross-functional and cross-component Scrum teams in areas deemed most conducive to success of the change. Each team should have the skills and empowerment to work on any aspect of the various technologies involved, along with the ability to perform all aspects of development, testing, release, and any other activities involved.

From my investigation of the pre-existing efforts, it had become clear the majority of the senior management had no real understanding of or exposure to healthy self-managing teams. Without that, it would be challenging to generate sufficient interest in more sustainable division-wide organizational change. Trent and I hoped a successful showcase Scrum team would help achieve greater buy-in.

But our *failure to address some of the structural forces eventually unraveled much of our earlier success.* Two large structural forces contributing to the unraveling were:

- Failure to adequately restructure reporting relationships tempted some managers to distract team members from their work.
- The new functionality built was ancillary to management's incentives, even though it produced tremendous savings for Nakashima as a whole.

The *Manifestation of Larman's First and Fifth Laws of Organizational Behavior* section covers these in more detail.

We initially established a single Scrum team focused on adding an end-to-end diagnostic capability to the MCS product. The end-to-end diagnostics showcase team is not the primary focus of this case study, although partial success in this effort helped open the door to the broader BIOS related efforts which are.

Because the end-to-end diagnostics efforts help to illuminate and foreshadow some of the challenges encountered in the BIOS efforts, the diagnostics team efforts are described in a little more detail later on.

LeSS-oriented Adoption within BIOS Group

The early success of the diagnostics team along with my continued socialization within the MCS division piqued the interest and eventual enrollment of Mitya, who was the director for the U.S.-based engineers in the BIOS group. The LeSS-oriented adoption within the BIOS group spearheaded by Mitya and myself is the primary focus of this case study.

The level of artificial self-inflicted complexity and the esoteric nature of the BIOS domain were such that a component boundary restricted to BIOS development alone still greatly benefited from a LeSS-oriented structure. It would help to resolve years of problematic practices.

The BIOS domain also provided a natural evolutionary path towards a full slice through the entire MCS system. The ability to quickly absorb a new generation of pre-production Intel CPUs into the MCS product prior to Intel's production launch of the CPUs is critical to maintain market relevance. This includes ensuring all required BIOS functionality works correctly on the pre-production CPUs, as well as ensuring any revisions and extensions of the blade architecture are working properly from a CPU integration perspective. Additionally, this includes ensuring all CPU administration services exposed at the MCS administration user interfaces are working, and have been extended to support new functionality Intel is introducing with the pre-production CPUs.

All of the above could be seen as a natural LeSS Huge Requirement Area for the MCS product as a whole.

The LeSS framework rules state each Requirement Area in a LeSS-Huge adoption should have the complete LeSS structure established "at the start". Although Mitya and I did completely restructure the U.S.-based members of the BIOS group from the start, better senior management alignment and buy-in would have made it possible to have started with a fuller, and more appropriate vertical slice of the product.

We started as best we could and then incrementally began expanding the BIOS component boundary upward through the various overall component layers. The *Feature Team Adoption Map for BIOS* in conjunction with the *Initial BIOS Component Boundary,* and *Expanded BIOS Multi-Component Boundary* diagrams illustrate this incremental expansion. The astute reader will notice this approach aligns with the *Feature Team Adoption Map* guide described in *Large-Scale Scrum: More with LeSS.*

The BIOS LeSS-oriented adoption efforts were hindered by a change in the Senior VP/GM, which occurred just around the time Mitya and I began our efforts. Had we retained the same level of executive support found with the original Senior VP/GM, far broader and more sustained success would likely have been achieved.

I learned a great deal from both the successes and failures of the LeSS-oriented adoption efforts within Nakashima's MCS division. Hopefully, this case study will help guide you in your journey as you learn from our successes and even more from our failures.

Initial Focus on Firmware Not Hardware Development

Historically the vast majority of the release schedule forecasting problems occurred in the firmware (e.g. BIOS, Network Interface Controller, Chassis Controller, etc.) and higher-level software (e.g. MCS Administrator, diagnostics, etc.) development aspects of the MCS product development group. Hardware development aspects tended to be far more predictable.

In practice, I only spent a small amount of time in conversations with people involved with designing manufacturing specifications for the external fabricators. Although expanding the LeSS adoption to include the engineers involved in hardware design would make sense in the long-term, it was not part of my initial focus.

In practice, neither the diagnostic nor BIOS teams I spent most of my time working with had much need to collaborate actively with the hardware engineers. Whenever a firmware developer had a need they would go over and talk with the hardware design engineers, it just didn't happen often. The MCS product was a relatively mature product by the time I was involved with the MCS division; as such most hardware design changes tended to be small and incremental. There was likely a potential opportunity to encourage greater innovation through more broadly cross-functional teams in the future with more tightly integrated hardware and firmware development.

Actual MCS Product Boundary

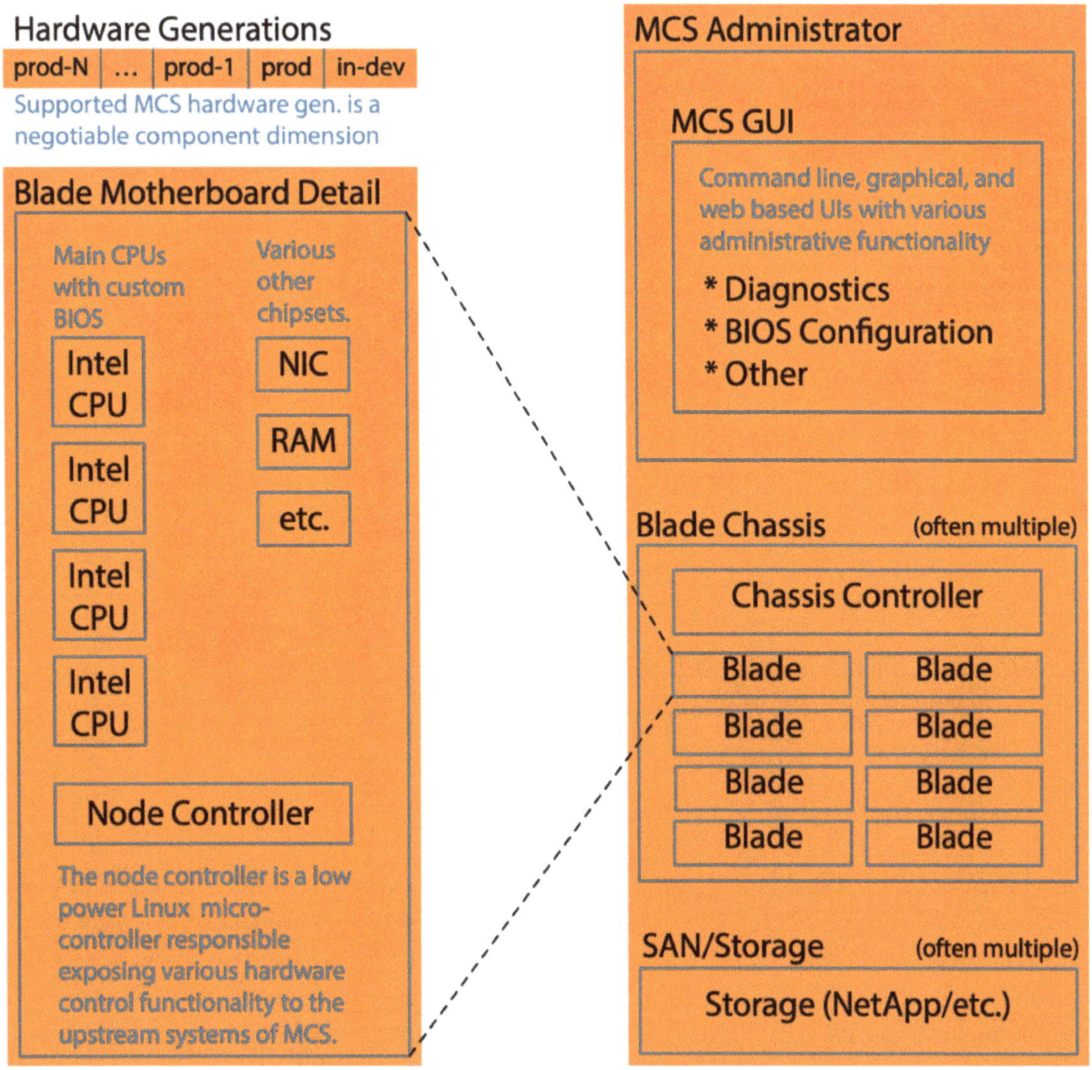

Figure 1: From the perspective of the Product Management group, Nakashima divisional boundaries, and external customers the natural product boundary includes the entire system of network, compute, and storage capability. Even broader product boundaries are possible but are not that practical as the coupling between other systems is sufficiently standardized to be interchangeable with data center hardware and software from a variety of vendors. These other systems do play a minor role in the larger scale testing scopes, but they are not the focus of Modular Compute System testing.

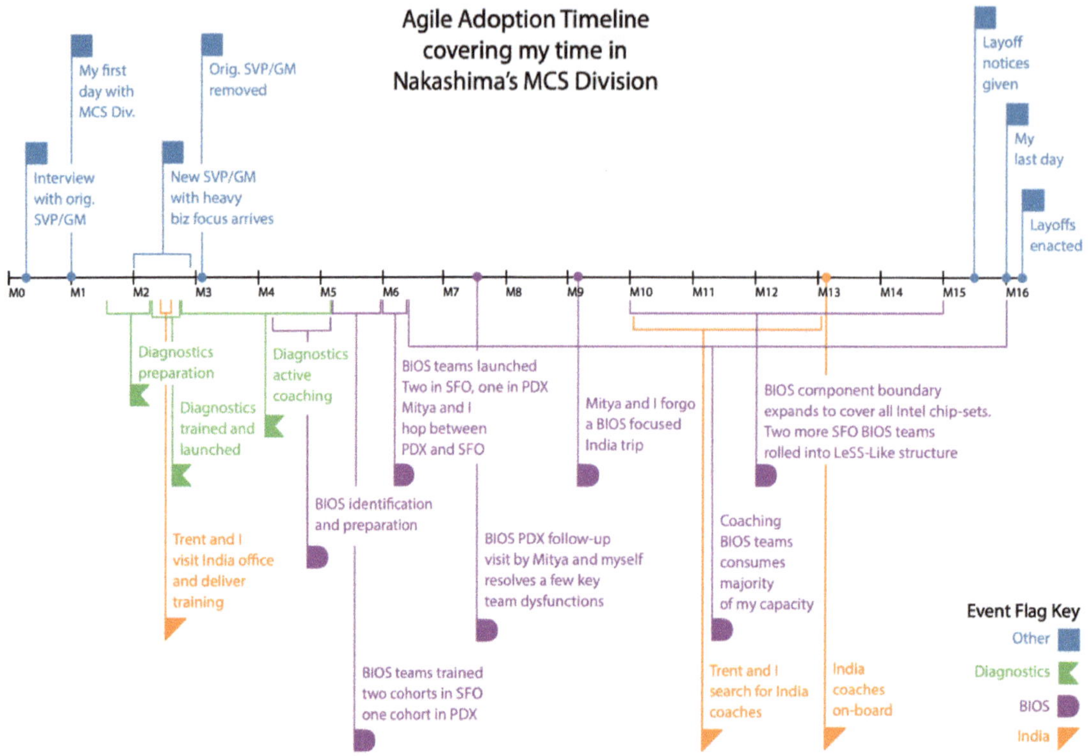

Figure 2: With the various overlapping adoption efforts and managerial changes it is easy to lose track of the overall story arch. Hopefully, this timeline will help you keep track.

Demonstrate Benefits of a Scrum Team

There was a great deal of initial skepticism within the MCS division that Scrum made sense within a hardware and firmware development effort. The thought being firmware and hardware efforts were somehow different from typical enterprise software development, and therefore not a good match for Scrum (ironic, as the original 1980s roots-of-Scrum research from Harvard involved hardware products). This perspective was reinforced by the fact that all the pre-existing 'agile' development efforts within MCS were not.

Considering the context, it made sense to apply the incremental LeSS-adoption Guide using a *Feature Team Adoption Map* to identify a meaningful multi-component boundary to stand-up a healthy Scrum team that could demonstrate useful results. This is to say it made sense to demonstrate the value of having a small team of people with all the skills to solve a problem, working directly with the customers who have the problem, and to have this team of people iteratively, adaptively, and incrementally solve the customer's problem.

We hoped to gain additional political capital by demonstrating:

- Scrum with firmware/hardware
- Self-managing team
- Improved customer collaboration

- Improved value delivery
- Impact of structure on culture
- Improved code quality
- Avoidance of the Contract Game

Desired Characteristics of Pilot Multi-Component

To achieve the demonstration objectives above, we needed to identify the right feature set of the MCS product for a pilot Scrum team to focus on. I recognized the chances of success would be greatest if we could identify a largely isolated and *decoupled set of multiple components which mapped significantly to a natural LeSS Huge Requirement Area* (RA) of the overall product. (Note that an RA is *not* defined by a component or architectural boundary, but sometimes there is a significant overlap of a functional RA and a body of related code, which in this early-step case was an advantage in simplifying the adoption).

The following criteria delineate the group of multiple components we were looking to identify. We wanted a group of components...

- Passing through "front to back" of MCS
- Appropriate to the capacity of a single team
- Providing meaningful value to customers
- Whose successful delivery would be politically difficult to ignore
- For which the team could be protected from delivery pressure
- With a codebase at least moderately decoupled from the rest of the MCS system, to avoid poor practices by an army of waterfall developers

Another criterion we could survive without but hoped to also find was:

- A group of components that could be released independently of the waterfall MCS releases; thereby providing faster feedback from real customers

Appropriate Diagnostics Feature Set Identified for Pilot Scrum team

It took some thoughtful discussion with Trent and others within the organization to find a good candidate set of components. The conclusion? A *diagnostic feature set* of MCS turned out to be a remarkably good choice since it satisfied every item on the list.

Tremendous financial savings in customer support costs and associated reputational benefits helped provide political air-cover while also generating enthusiastic support from the field support division. The diagnostic feature set was the only obvious feature set meeting our criteria, yet the fit was fantastic!

Components Affected by Diagnostic Feature Set

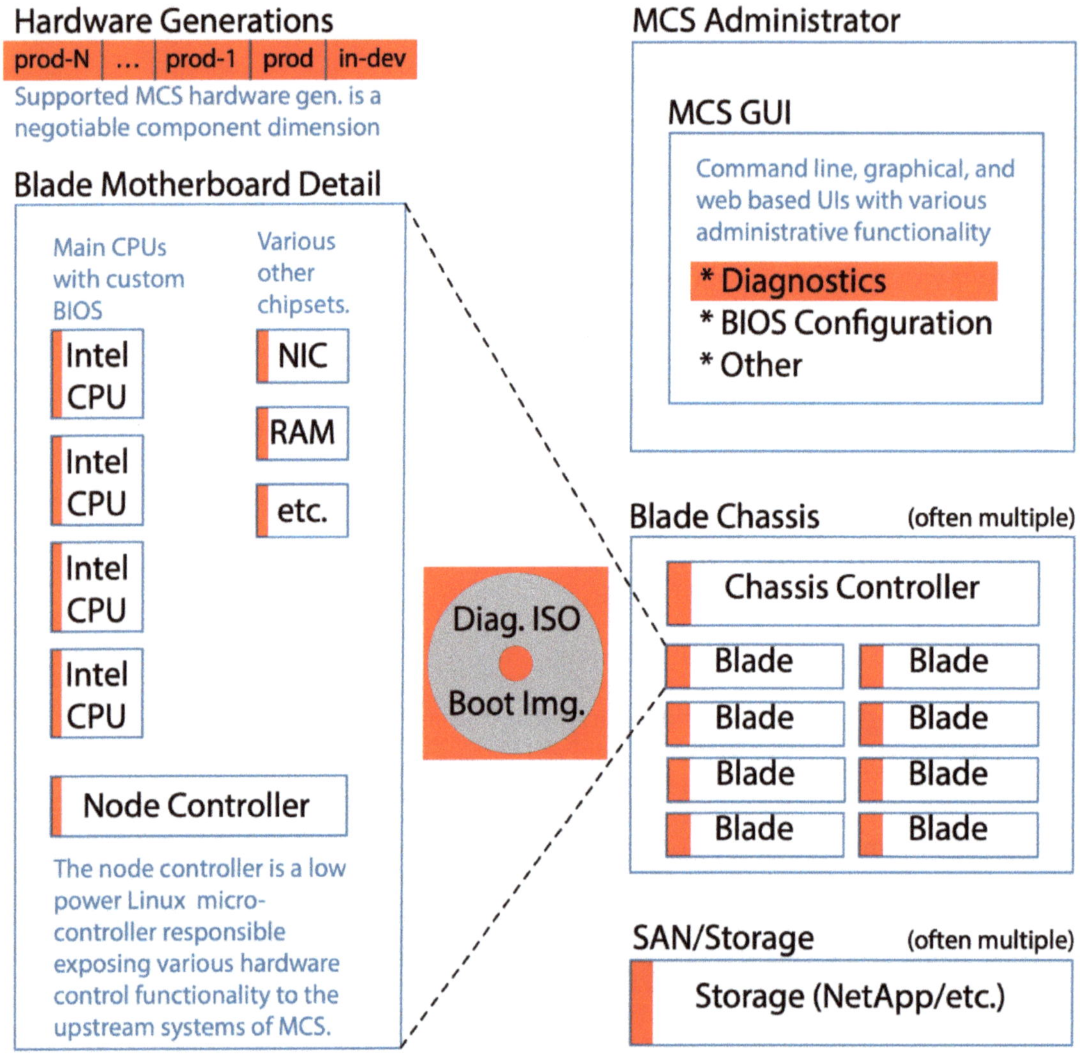

Figure 3: Although the diagnostic code is largely encapsulated in a custom ISO image and some diagnostic focused code in the MCSA, the diagnostics capabilities are broadly focused and relevant to all hardware generations. Detailed knowledge of each component in the entire MCS system is often required. When a given MCS component's firmware is missing the ability to probe it, the diagnostic team adds it.

Feature Team Adoption Map for Diagnostic Team

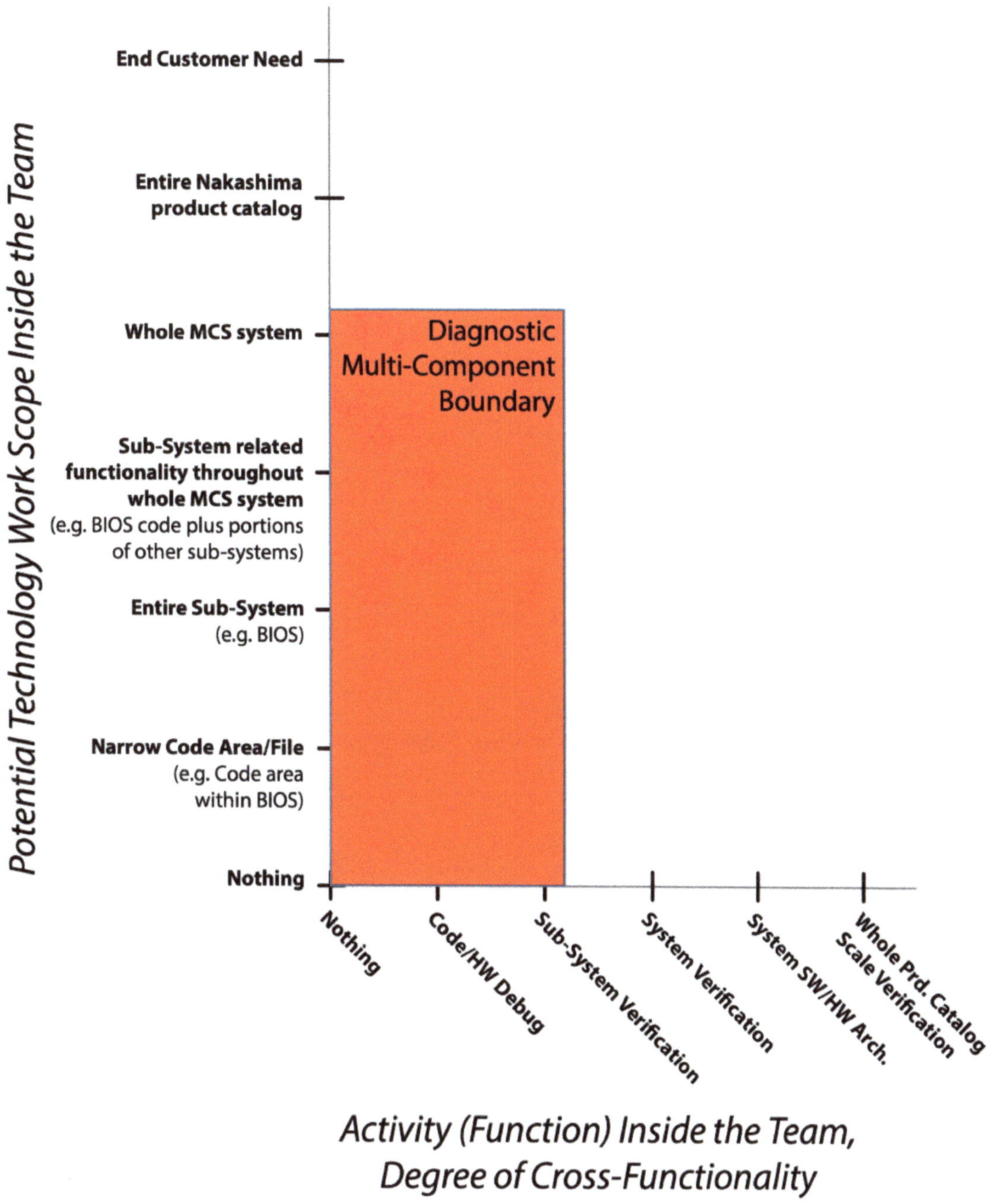

Figure 4: The diagnostic capability is narrowly focused on helping customers diagnose problems with their on-site MCS systems, particularly hardware component failures. Although the focus is narrow, the scope spans the whole MCS system. More information on the usage of Feature Team Adoption maps can be found at: https://less.works/less/adoption/feature-team-adoption_map

Diagnostics Team Behavioral Achievements

From the initial launch onward people began to behave differently than before. After four or five Sprints changed behaviors included ...

- Active collaboration between the entire diagnostics Scrum team and engineers in the field support division
- A team that worked collaboratively rather than as individuals, incrementally adjusted and improved their practices each Sprint, always produced shippable component increments, and established rich direct collaborative relationships with the key stakeholders
- A Multi-Component Backlog ordering heavily influenced by metrics the field support and another collaborating division were able to produce. These metrics made it possible to assign an estimated monthly cost of delay for most diagnostic capabilities we had conceptualized. The projected savings of the higher priority diagnostic capabilities were *staggering*!

Diagnostics Team Technical Achievements

An explicit and expanding Definition of Done, effective Scrum events, a small amount of technical coaching, and avoiding the Contract Game combined to make a huge difference in technical practices.

Within four or five Sprints the following were readily observable:

- Automated unit testing in any portions of the MCS C++ and Python code the diagnostics Scrum team touched
- Automated unit test practices were acting as a forcing function for better crafted and less troublesome code for all of the diagnostics specific code and portions of the overall MCS codebase
- Active development of improved and broader automated integration tests than previously existed for the MCS system

Diagnostics Team Launch Steps

There was no mystery to our success. Steps included:

- Applied the LeSS guide *Temporary Fake Product Owner* for the diagnostic multi-component to identify a personality conducive to supporting and guiding the team, who had enough positional and political influence for his decisions to be respected by the various stakeholders.
    - This person was a *fake* Product Owner because they still had to play the *Contract Game*, doing requirements and conforming to milestones as directed by others in the company.

- Assembled an eight-member development team with all the software and test engineering skills needed (or learned) to work across the various MCS subsystems required.
- Took full-time possession of a mid-sized meeting room for use as the development team's co-located working space.
- I delivered a couple of days of formal classroom training for all Scrum team members, as well as key stakeholders.
- We conducted a collaborative chartering effort consisting of a couple of days of dedicated chartering meetings, along with a variety of preliminary and follow-up meetings. This helped achieve overall alignment between and within the stakeholders and Scrum team members.
- I provided active executive, process, and technical coaching for the first few Sprints before refocusing most of my efforts on the upcoming LeSS-oriented adoption in the MCS division's BIOS group.

See the *Getting Started* guide in *Large-Scale Scrum: More with LeSS* for additional guidance on launching teams. Although written from the perspective of launching multiple teams within a LeSS structure, it is just as applicable to launching a single pilot Scrum team.

Diagnostics Team Photos and Artifacts

Figure 5: Here is a photo of the diagnostics Scrum development team. Pairing and swarming became more common over time, though full mob programming never quite caught on. The team had both the test and development talent needed to deliver a potentially shippable increment at the end of each Sprint. The development team used a physical task board. The meeting room we took over was a bit smaller than we would have liked.

Second Definition of Done (Firmware Feature Team in Waterfall Ecosystem)

Version: 2.03

Date: July 5, 2017

Common

- ❑ Zero bugs at the end of the Sprint within the Dev team's control to fix.
- ❑ Any similar functionality between the stand-alone and integrated solution has been factored into common shared libraries.
- ❑ Manually validated against each available hardware platform profile.
- ❑ Release notes updated and published to common location.
- ❑ Configuration information and Release note information saved in source control in a manner which makes it easy for the technical writing team to write documentation for the release.
- ❑ Peer Review completed. (Pair programming counts as peer review.)
- ❑ Demo to Product Owner

Specific to Stand-alone Solution

- ❑ Automated unit test created for both positive and negative cases for any new or modified functionality within custom code. Not required for third-party libraries developed outside the team.
- ❑ Manual Regression executed and passed for all platforms.
- ❑ Passed all solution level test cases for new defects (manual testing today).
- ❑ Final release image build by centralized build systems team is successful.
- ❑ Optimal image size should not increase beyond 100MB.

Specific to Larger Solution

- ❑ Code committed to main branch of overall solution.
- ❑ Automated smoke tests extended to cover any new or modified functionality.
- ❑ Existing commit tests pass.
- ❑ No new static analysis errors introduced.
- ❑ Manual feature test passed.
- ❑ No relevant open defects.
- ❑ No relevant open regression defects.

Figure 6: The Definition of Done used by the diagnostics team evolved to what you see here after a few Sprints. The stand-alone portion of the Increment was provided to the field service division by the end of each Sprint. Providing the MCS integrated diagnostics capabilities to the end customer required waiting for a release of the waterfall developed MCS product. This example Definition of Done along with additional context can be found in Table 9.2 of Forging Change.

Diagnostics Team Culturally Relevant Elements

A few cultural observations concerning the pilot effort are listed below. Many of these cultural observations are also relevant to a better understanding of the subsequent LeSS-oriented adoption in the BIOS group.

Manifestation of Larman's First and Fifth Laws of Organizational Behavior

The first and fifth of Larman's Laws of Organizational Behavior are:

- **Organizations are implicitly optimized to avoid changing the status quo middle- and first-level manager and "specialist" positions & power structures.**
- **(in large established orgs) Culture follows structure. And in tiny young orgs, structure follows culture.**

All five of Larman's Laws of Organizational Behavior can be found on the structure page of the LeSS website at.

Even within the small diagnostics pilot Scrum team, the first and fifth laws were clearly on display. The positive changes in effective structure and resulting culture were limited to the diagnostic team and the stakeholders with whom the diagnostic team actively collaborated. In contrast, the status quo in the majority of the middle management layer remained largely unchanged.

The diagnostic team's expanded component boundary cut across many different components within the MCS system. Each of these components typically had its own set of engineers along with a manager per geographic region, rolling up into one of two VPs. The diagnostics development team was formed by having each of the relevant managers fully allocate a software or test engineer with knowledge of the relevant components. Given the delivery pressure of the overall waterfall efforts, managers were very reluctant to allocate people to the diagnostics team. They ultimately only did so at the behest of the original Sr. VP.

Once the Scrum team was up and running, it took a great deal of political pressure as well as a formal directive from the original Sr. VP before the first and second level managers stopped attempting to task individual diagnostics development team members with unrelated work. Some of the development team members eventually had to be formally assigned to a manager related to the diagnostics effort to stop some problems.

Just as Larman's Laws of Organizational Behavior would predict, having the Scrum development team members report to engineering managers who concurrently experienced delivery pressures from the overall MCS product was very problematic. Although the Sr. VP mitigated this problem by being supportive, the organizational chart was never fully flattened. Many of the development team members still continued to report up through one of the VPs who never fully embraced the changes. The only reporting changes involved related to which director was responsible for some of the diagnostics Scrum development team members.

Contrast with LeSS Book Guidance

At first glance, the diagnostic pilot aligns with the *Parallel Organizations* guide in the third LeSS book, *Large-Scale Scrum*. Regrettably, there are at least a couple of pernicious differences.

When describing the parallel organization strategy Larman and Vodde list a few caveats. The first caveat listed is:

> A parallel organization is not a pilot, and one consequence is that the line of organizational reporting must be separate from the traditional organization.

The effective team level structure of the diagnostic team was radically changed and aligned with Scrum, yet the formal organizational reporting relationships remained. This failure left the team overly vulnerable to change in the executive management layer.

Even though the diagnostic team was never subject to the Contract Game, the diagnostic team members still reported up through middle managers who were engaged in the Contract Game for the overall waterfall efforts. As the middle managers became increasingly desperate for more development capacity to throw on the bonfire of an upcoming waterfall release they increasingly resumed their earlier behaviors of redirecting the efforts of individual diagnostic team members. Although the original engineering SVP/GM had actively protected the diagnostic team from such dysfunctions, as soon as he departed the legacy status quo began to incrementally erode the supportive context that had enabled the diagnostic team's early success.

The second key difference is the diagnostic team was seen as a showcase rather than as the first of many teams that would eventually form a parallel organization. In other words, the diagnostic effort was not seen as the first step in executing a committed collective decision by senior management to slowly migrate all of MCS development into a LeSS-oriented structure.

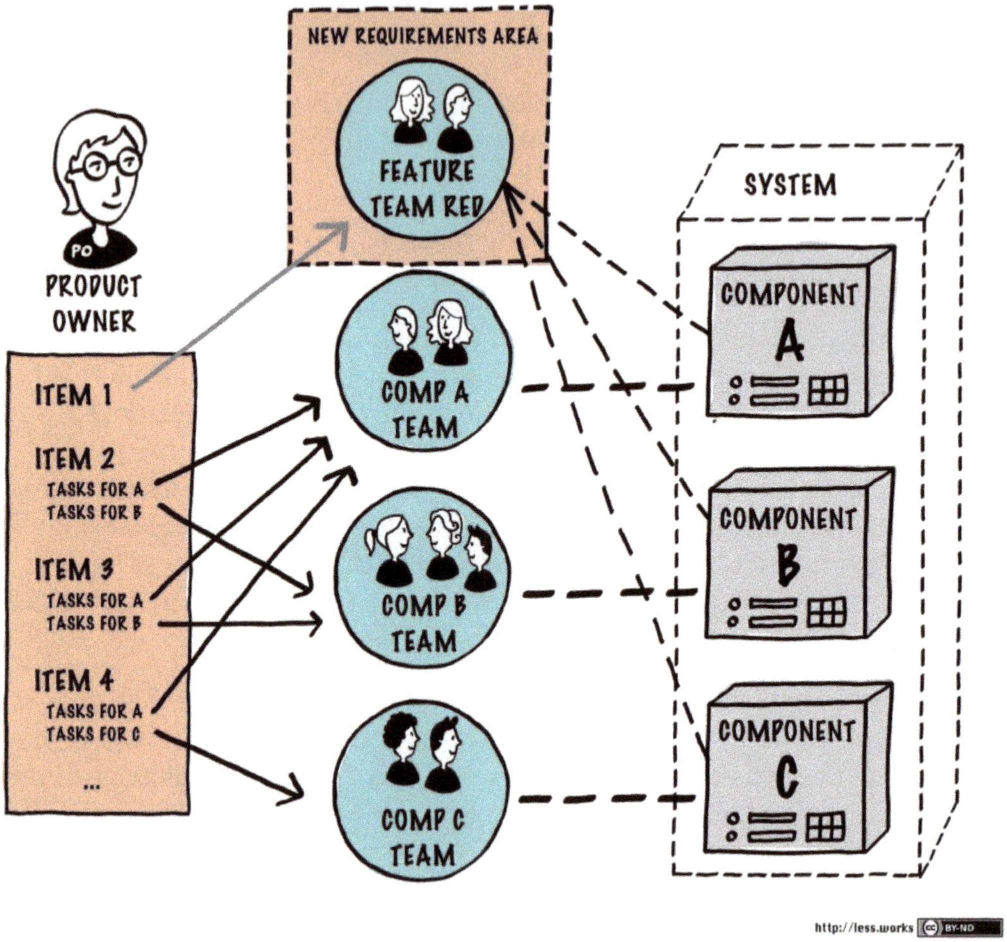

Figure 7: You will find this diagram as Figure 4.11 in Large-Scale Scrum: More with LeSS as part of the Transitioning to Feature Teams guide. You will notice Feature Team Red in its newly formed Requirement Area consumes from the same Product Backlog as do all the component teams. Although this loosely correlates to the diagnostic team situation, the day to day reality was slightly different. The diagnostic team was a real self-managing team free from the negative direct effects of the Contract Game. In contrast, most of the other MCS teams were subject to the Contract Game within a waterfall delivery context. The diagnostic team's organizational reporting relationships were never changed so as to intersect the organizational chart above the level at which the Contract Game was being played for the waterfall teams. This failure eventually resulted in the erosion of the supportive context required for the diagnostic team to remain successful. This failure became increasingly apparent after the departure of the original engineering SVP/GM.

Relevant References

The most up to date version of the LeSS rules can be found on the LeSS website

The following LeSS Rule seems particularly relevant:

- *"LeSS Rule: For the product group, establish the complete LeSS structure "at the start"; this is vital for a LeSS adoption."*

We clearly didn't achieve this since only one team was set up. Although the diagnostics team level structure was created from the start, we didn't manage to change the reporting relationships and flatten out the org chart as it pertained to the diagnostics team.

Large-Scale Scrum: More with Less provides the following relevant guides:

- *Guide: Build Team-Based Organizations*: Pay particular focus to the parts of this guide dealing with having stable organizations over dynamic matrixed structures.
- *Guide: LeSS Organizational Structure*: Includes the following quote: "LeSS organizations don't have matrix structures and there are no dotted-line managers."
- *Guide: Transitioning to Feature Teams:* Provides a high-level overview of various transition strategies.
- *Guide: One Requirement Area at a Time*: Details an incremental approach to LeSS Huge adoptions.
- *Guide: Parallel Organizations*: Details the creation of a separate organization as an adoption strategy. The caveats listed are particularly insightful.
- *Guide: Feature Team Adoption Maps*: Provides more insight into visualizing the gradual expansion of feature team responsibility as demonstrated in Figure 4 above.
- *Guide: Evolve the Definition of Done*: Explains how a Definition of Done can be used to more explicitly visualize incremental improvement and its relevance to various stakeholders.
- *Guide: Getting Started:* Just as applicable to launching an individual team as a set of teams.

Reflections on Executive Layer Changes

Although the new SVP was extremely talented in his own way and moderately technically savvy, he lacked the engineering insight of the short-tenured chief engineer style SVP he replaced.

The existing senior management reporting into the SVP lacked real-world exposure to anything like a proper agile team with good software engineering practices. Without such exposure, it was difficult to obtain support for even greater change.

Failure to avoid the Contract Game and a desire for self-preservation of the status quo power structures made it hard for many to appreciate or accept the improvements which were made over time. This is exactly as the first of the aforementioned *Larman's Laws of Organizational Behavior* predicts.

Had I the wisdom and skill at the time to recognize the need for and to conduct an executive workshop comparable to a *Certified LeSS for Executives* course focused on helping senior management to own rather than rent the change, things might have gone differently. Had I done this when I still had the original SVP to support me, the original SVP might have been seen as making enough drastic changes to have survived the political forces at play above the divisional layer.

If nothing else, an executive workshop coupled with an informed consent workshop may have helped highlight passive aggressive behaviors by the software VP.

Driving greater awareness of the magnitude of structural organizational change required for sustainable cultural change would run the risk of shutting down any improvement efforts before being able to make the incremental gains which were made. Yet, had the original SVP been willing to commit to a LeSS-oriented adoption after such an executive workshop it would have been even harder to reverse the adoption efforts.

By the time the new SVP showed up, the die leading to the massive layoffs and destruction of many meaningful improvements had already been cast. I just didn't know it yet, and wouldn't for another year.

There was still great benefit to what was achieved. The diagnostic functionality put in place by the pilot diagnostics team continues to save millions in return costs. It is unlikely any diagnostics capability of comparable quality would have been achievable within the legacy organizational structure. The even greater positive impact of many of the improvements in the BIOS production code, BIOS test infrastructure, and organizational norms within the BIOS teams obtained far too much momentum to ever be fully reversed.

Enlightened minds never again see the world the same. Similarly, improvements ingrained in the code of a production product tend to last for decades.

BIOS Management Interest

As the diagnostics Scrum team began to gel, I began looking for another area of the MCS landscape to focus on. I again leveraged Trent's knowledge of organizational dynamics. As before, we wanted to gradually transition to feature teams while focusing on areas with fully enrolled management support. Given the effectiveness of the diagnostic Scrum team efforts, a somewhat broader scope had become more tenable. That said I was still the only coach, and there was not enough funding for additional coaching capacity at the time.

There was a director, Mitya Dubinksy, who although initially somewhat skeptical, expressed interest in what benefit might be possible. Over the course of a few weeks, I was able to bring Mitya further along in his thought processes. I was assisted in this effort by a peer of Mitya named Krishna Mishra. Krishna played a key role in the diagnostics pilot Scrum team effort. Krishna also happened to manage a group of engineers who frequently interacted with Mitya's group.

Mitya's group was responsible for providing a customized BIOS for MCS. BIOS is the firmware used to perform hardware initialization of a compute node (blade) during the booting process. It also provides runtime services to whichever operating system happens to be running on a compute node within MCS. In the case of MCS and competing products, a custom BIOS is part of what makes it possible to remotely administer each node's hardware settings without having to physically access the hardware. The access is particularly important when you realize the hardware is often in a distant lightly staffed server farm.

BIOS Overview

The custom BIOS code was easily the most challenging and specialized software development aspect of the entire overall MCS system. Much of the remaining systems were comprised of C++, Java, and Python middleware running on mature chipsets and running within stripped-down Linux operating systems on dedicated appliance hardware. Some of these systems required contending with low power and memory constraints, yet that was nothing compared to what the BIOS engineers had to deal with. In spite of all this, the BIOS group was the one with management expressing the greatest eagerness to change and improve.

Market viability demands Nakashima develop custom BIOS releases quickly enough to keep pace with Intel's processor releases. Even with AMI providing the base of the BIOS firmware, historically poor engineering practices and lack of cross-functional multi-learning teams meant it still took a group of forty or more highly specialized hardware, software, and test engineers working on the custom MCS BIOS to keep current with Intel.

Although major BIOS releases tend to correspond with an overall MCS release, smaller independent BIOS releases also happen on occasion. The smaller independent releases are generally motivated by minor Intel hardware revisions or minor updates in the AMI codebase on which the custom MCS BIOS is based.

In consideration of the eagerness for change within the BIOS management reporting line, and the lack-luster support from the Software VP, the sensible thing was to pursue the art of the possible within the influence of the Hardware VP and Quality Assurance VP. We decided to define a component boundary constrained to the custom BIOS alone, and then slowly expand the boundary as the BIOS teams matured.

At a macro level the BIOS is merely one component of the overall MCS system, yet at a micro level every bit of a LeSS-oriented structure remains fully relevant. The BIOS component is itself composed of a very large set of sub-components which are beyond the scope of this document.

The MCS division has somewhere on the order of a few thousand engineers all focused on various aspects of the MCS product. Starting with a broader expanded BIOS multi-component boundary before first improving the engineering practices and cross-training within the scope of the BIOS component teams would have been problematic. The engineering practices throughout MCS were relatively abysmal, just as you might expect from years of playing the Contract Game. There were more than enough quality problems and engineering silos within the initial BIOS component boundary to consume all the coaching focus we had available to provide.

LeSS advises to have coaching on three levels (organizational, team, and technical) as explained here, and I was covering all three of them. I helped Trent interview and recruit a couple of coaches in Bengaluru, yet I was the only agile coach the MCS division had in the western hemisphere. Had we not lost the original engineering SVP/GM within the first two and half months of my tenure, the coaching capacity situation would have likely been different. With the new engineering SVP/GM looking to downsize the division and not fully understanding the agile adoption effort, we were lucky to have the coaching capacity we did.

BIOS Expanded From the Bottom Up

As explained in LeSS:

There are roughly two approaches to LeSS Huge adoption:

1. One Requirement Area at a time
2. Gradually expanding the work-scope of the team, Definition of Done and the Product Definition

— from here

We followed the 2nd approach, although the first one: One Requirement Area at a time would have meant more impactful organizational change.

The BIOS LeSS-oriented adoption was not directly driven by the principle of being customer-centric with a whole-product focus. Rather the mechanics of a LeSS-oriented structure were seen as a solution for solving many of the transparency, coordination, and quality issues the BIOS teams were facing.

The benefits of working towards an expanded BIOS multi-component boundary until it aligned with a natural feature set of the MCS product were not initially clear to the BIOS teams or management, yet they became so over time. The increased awareness was driven by a variety of factors including: improved transparency of the impediments caused by dealing with dependencies outside of the BIOS teams, effective retrospectives resulting in meaningful experiments within each new Sprint, and continued coaching on my part. More detail is provided in the *BIOS Component Boundary Expands* section later on.

Oddly, the expanded multi-component boundary of the LeSS teams started deep within an esoteric component of the overall product architecture, and then slowly expanded upwards towards the user interface. Although this is an unusual and less than ideal place for a LeSS adoption to start, it was where management buy-in and interest for change was found. It is remarkable how much can be accomplished simply by enabling the creative potential of teams, even with less than ideal starting conditions.

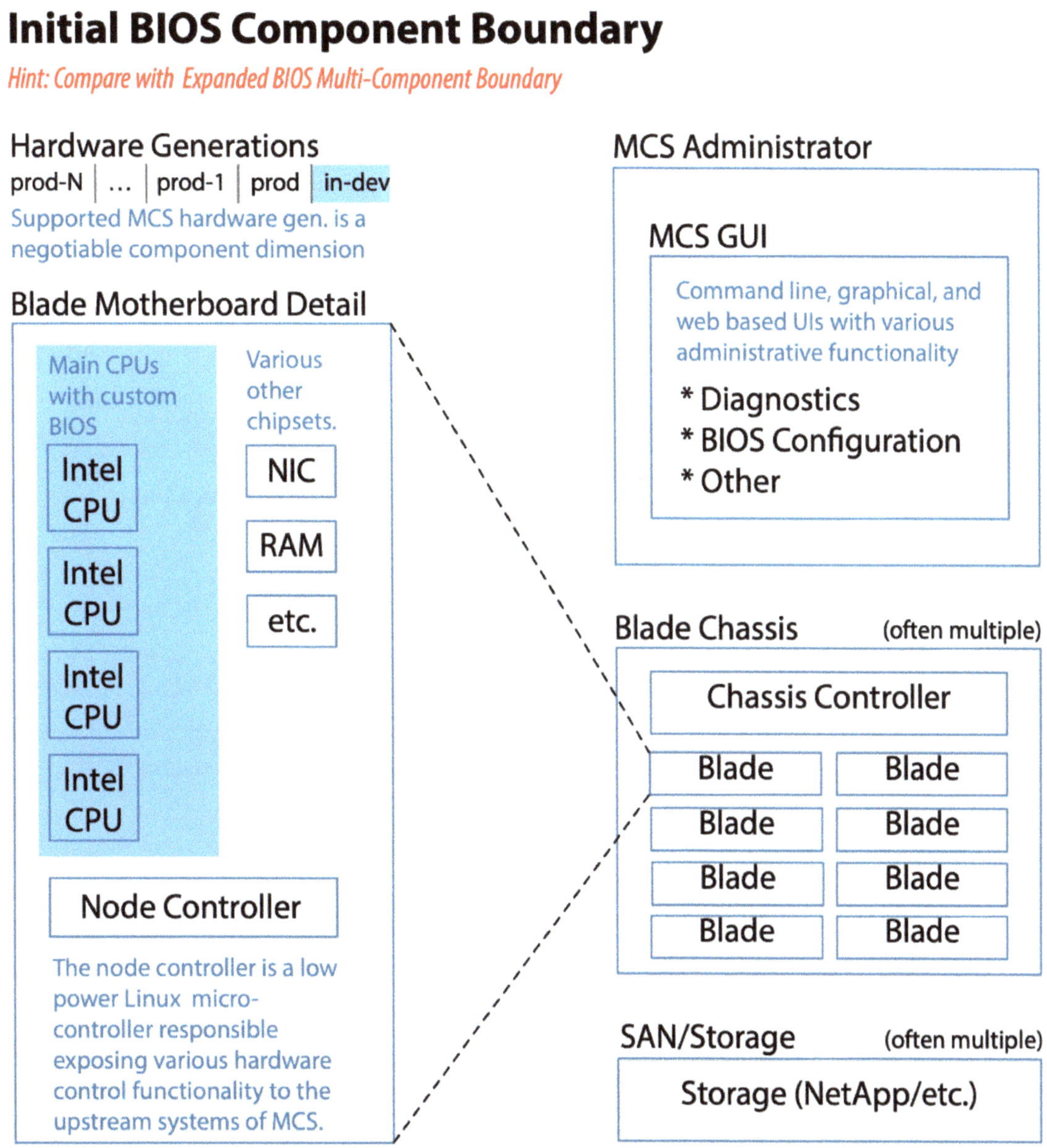

Figure 8: The initial BIOS component boundary only included the custom BIOS. Even at this narrower scope, it still included hundreds of specialized code areas within the custom BIOS itself and millions of lines of C code. Few if any of the several dozen BIOS engineers initially knew more than one or two aspects of the BIOS code.

Expanded BIOS Multi-Component Boundary

Hint: Compare with Initial BIOS Component Boundary

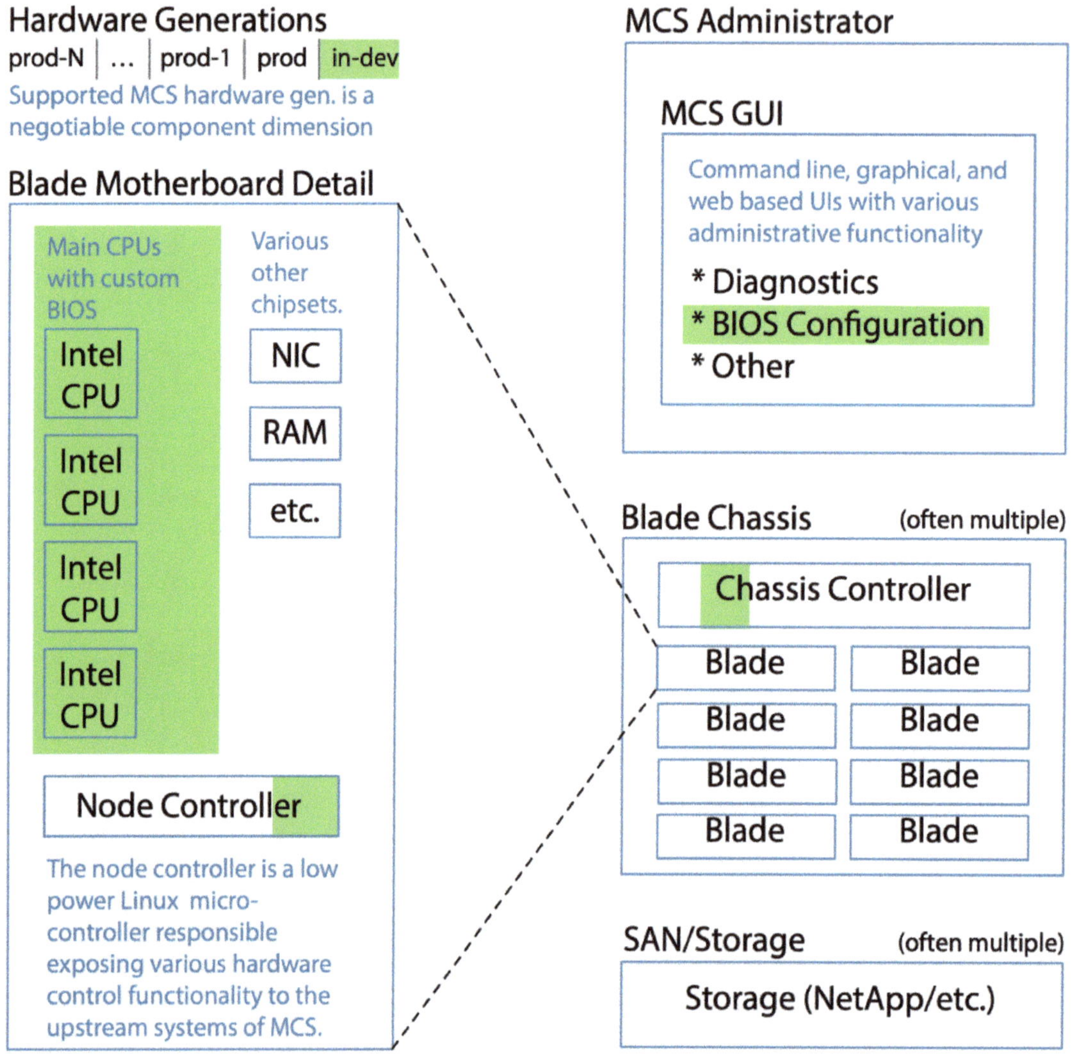

Figure 9: The expanded BIOS multi-component boundary included everything along the BIOS configuration control path. It mapped to a natural product requirement area, and could be easily understood by a Product Owner from the Product Management group. Although never fully realized, efforts to move in this direction were made.

Feature Team Adoption Map for BIOS Teams

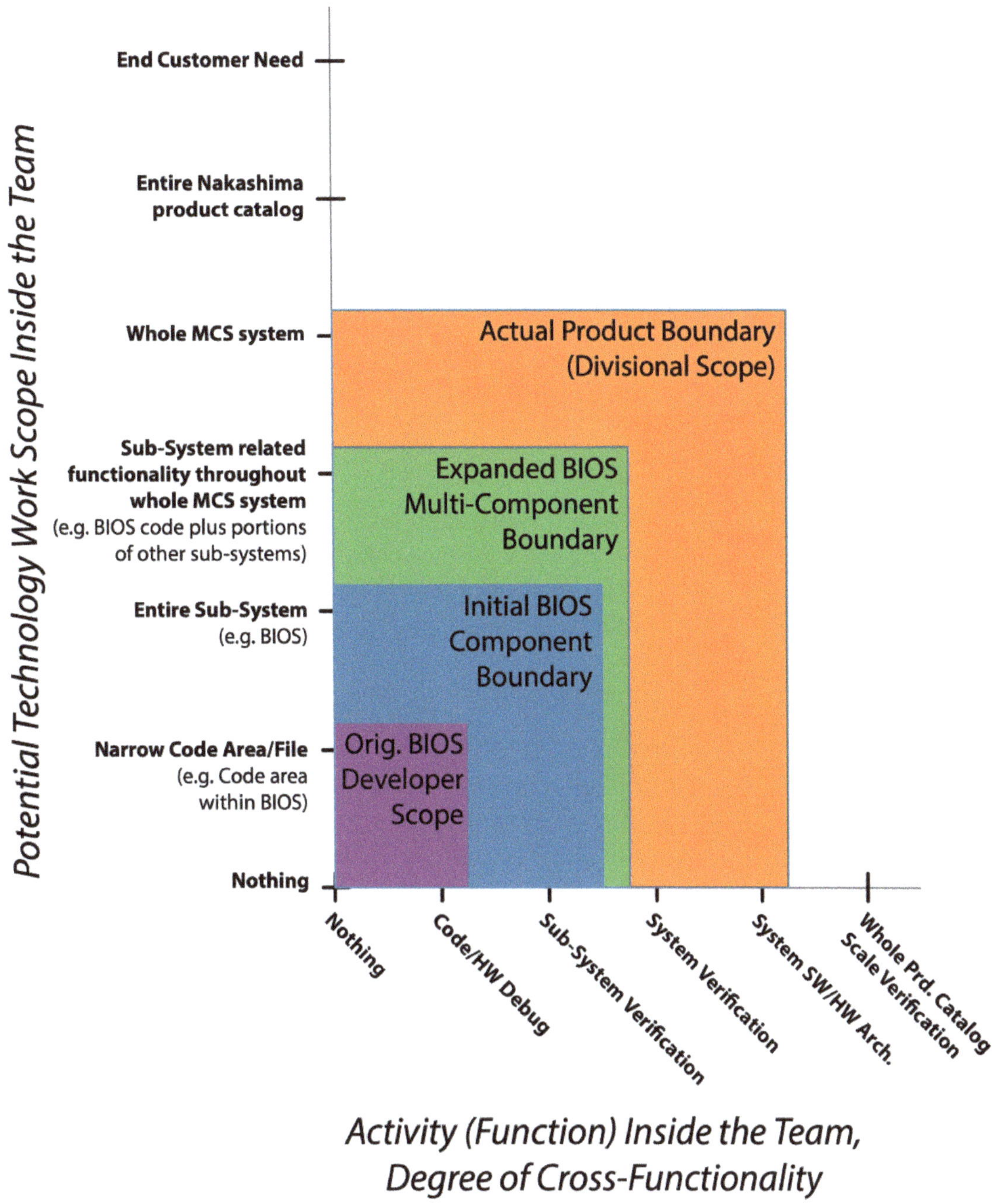

Figure 10: The BIOS developers were originally more of a loose group of a few dozen individuals who each specialized in a narrow aspect of the BIOS customization. The BIOS system alone contained millions of lines of code in an extremely esoteric system domain.

"In-Between" BIOS Teams

It is a little challenging to select a good adjective for the newly formed BIOS teams.

The newly formed BIOS teams were vastly more ***cross-functional*** than the legacy BIOS teams. Each team was responsible and capable of the authorship and end-to-end testing of any BIOS changes.

The newly formed BIOS teams were also ***self-managing*** and ***co-located*** from the start. Though due to the layoffs and other organizational churn they were not as ***long-lived*** as Mitya and I intended.

The *Feature Team Adoption Maps* guide in *Large-Scale Scrum* provides several useful definitions for describing teams. Two are:

> **Extended component teams**—Any team that has a limited component work scope yet is responsible for checking that their part works within the larger product is an extended component team.
>
> **Feature teams**—Any team that has a whole-product focus and is involved from clarifying customer-centric features to testing them is a feature team. Feature teams also exist along a scale. They can be limited to just implementing the features stated they need. Or, when the product definition is broad enough, they can be involved with identifying and solving the customers' real problems and thus co-creating the product on the whole system.

The newly structured BIOS teams were capable of acting as *extended component teams* from their formation. They had the capability and responsibility of performing end-to-end testing on any changes they made. The *testing* extended from the MCS GUI (whose code they did not write), through the Chassis Controller (whose code they did not write), through the Node Controller (whose code they did not write), and finally ending in the BIOS code running on the Intel CPUs. In contrast, the *coding* of the newly structured BIOS teams initially was only within the *Initial BIOS Component Boundary* detailed in Figure 8. As you can see this aligns perfectly with the definition of an *extended component team*.

The newly structured BIOS teams failed to initially meet the definition of a *feature team*. To become *feature teams* would require including all relevant code front-to-back. Although the BIOS teams never quite achieved this during my time with Nakashima's MCS division, they were making progress.

In summary the newly structured BIOS teams:

1. Started as *extended component teams* which were *self-managing* and *co-located*.
2. Aimed to become *component-expanded teams* to cover more components along the communication path between the BIOS component and the MCS GUI component.
3. Planned to become *feature teams* by expanding their responsibility to "everything" needed to deliver end-to-end features.

BIOS Organizational Context

The BIOS LeSS-oriented adoption occurred during a period of active churn in the executive layers. When the BIOS adoption was started the VP in charge of all the Hardware development was very supportive, as were a variety of other VPs throughout the organization. This was sufficient to make the initial adoption efforts possible and successful in the short run. As both the SVP and VP level management changed we lost much of the support needed, even though our efforts were widely regarded as successful by most people involved. Ambivalence by a new SVP along with the loss of the supportive Hardware VP coupled with massive layoffs ultimately eroded our progress. The following series of organizational chart diagrams help to highlight the situation.

Original Organizational Structure with Original SVP

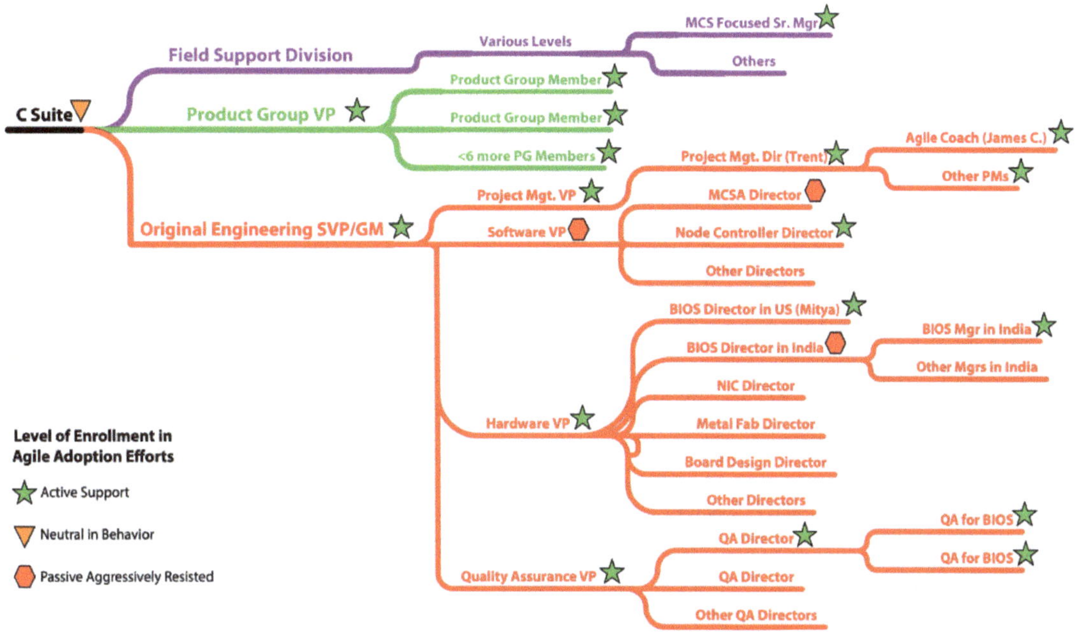

Figure 11: The initial Sr. VP/GM of engineering for the MCS division was extremely supportive of the agile adoption efforts. I also found active support throughout much of the organization. A large number of directors, managers, and individual contributors provided active guidance as I attempted to better understand and help the organization. Unfortunately, this Sr. VP's tenure was very short and there was a key VP responsible for the more pure software portions of the product who was passively aggressively opposed to any real change.

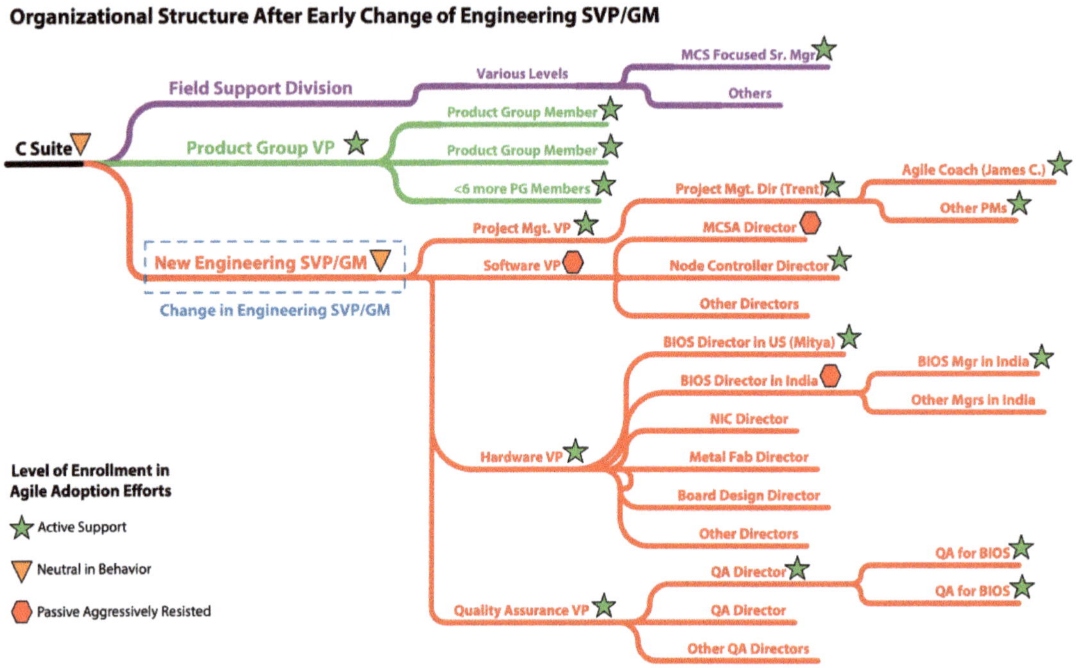

Figure 12: The initial Sr. VP/GM of engineering of the MCS Division only had his role for a few months before I arrived. Within a couple months of my arrival he was replaced with another Sr. VP. In retrospect it is obvious the new Sr. VP's direction from the C suite was to rationalize the size of the division. The new Sr. VP was almost completely unavailable to me and unwilling to actively engage in the agile transformation efforts. Although it generally happened outside of my view, I believe I continued to receive active support and air cover from the Project Management VP. Although there were some additional organizational changes over time once the new engineering SVP took over, none were very significant to the teams attempting an agile adoption until the Hardware VP left.

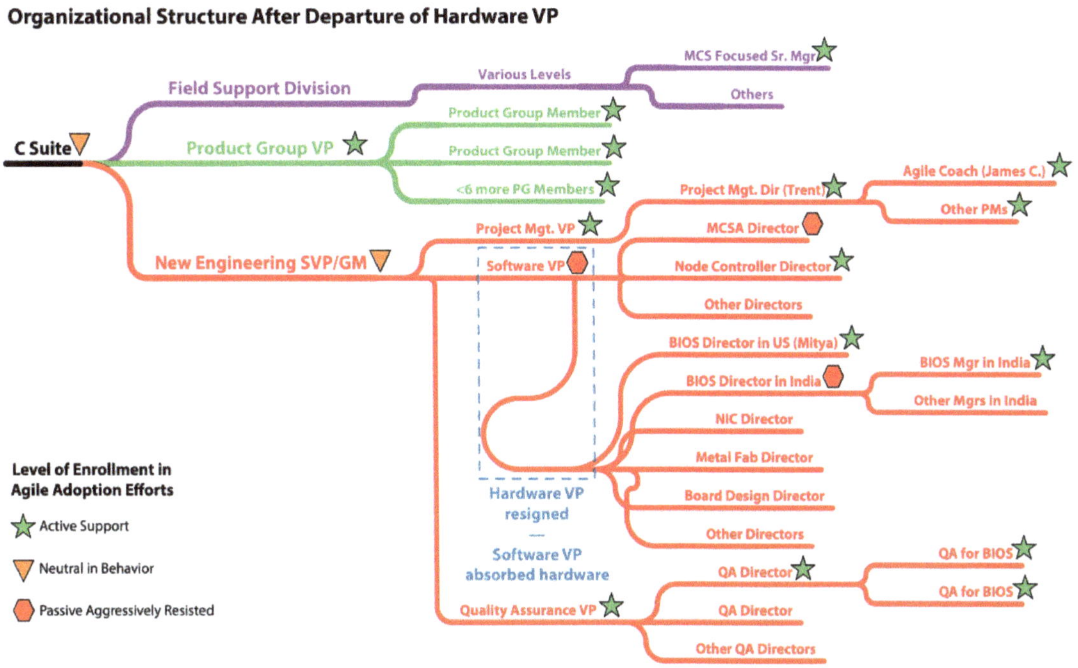

Figure 13: Under the cloud of upcoming and active layoffs many people began to depart the organization voluntarily. Around the same time a new extremely well funded startup began to actively recruit some of the more skillful engineers and managers in the MCS division. One of these departures was the Hardware VP who the BIOS teams had reported through. The new engineering SVP chose not to backfill the Hardware VP but instead to have all those previously reporting up through the Hardware VP report through the Software VP. As the Software VP was always passively aggressively working against the agile adoption efforts this did not bode well. Over the course of a few months half the BIOS team members were laid off, my engagement ended, and Mitya followed the Hardware VP to the same well funded startup the Hardware VP had left for. A little over a year later, Trent also left Nakashima Incorporated.

BIOS Component Boundaries and Geography

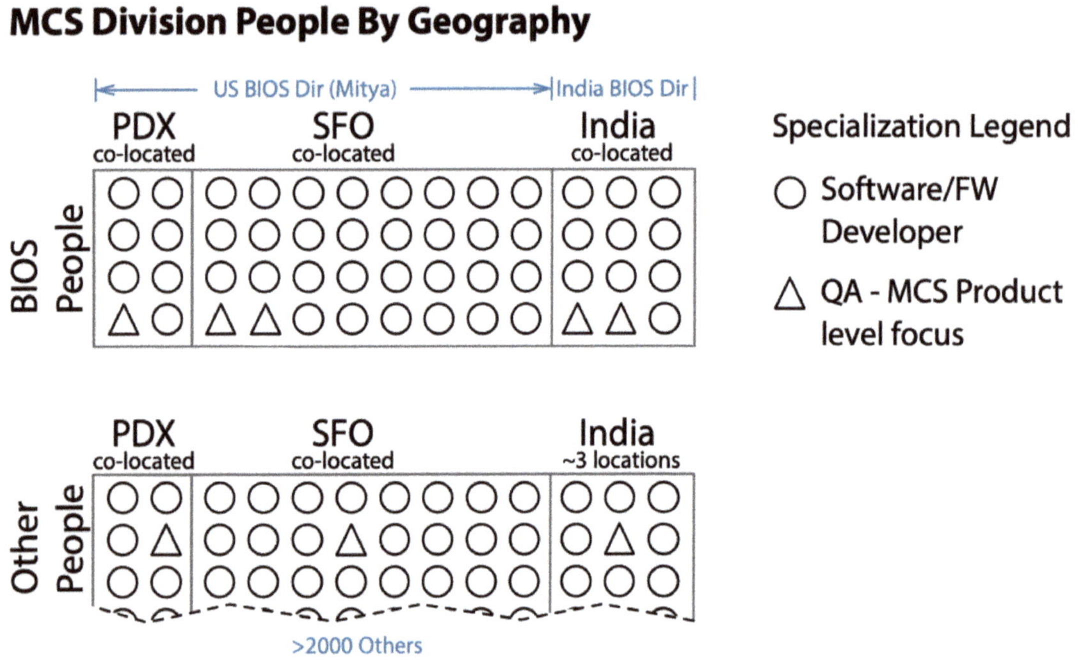

Figure 14: The vast majority of the people within the MCS Division are co-located on one or two floors within a single building in their respective cities. We were careful to ensure BIOS team members were generally sitting within a few feet of their teammates. Workstations were generally friendly to swarming. Half the work occurred in lab space so many team members effectively had two working locations. With the exception of a handful of the testing specialists, everyone in the US reported through Mitya. Even the testing specialists were co-located, fully allocated to BIOS, and treated just like everyone else on the teams. There were one or two BIOS developers who were dispersed but these were the only exceptions. Unfortunately, we didn't manage to officially remove specialist manager roles as part of a matrix structure. Nevertheless, managers didn't emphasize or hold onto specialism but supported people being multi-skilled.

BIOS Extended Component Team Expansion
By MCS Hardware Generation

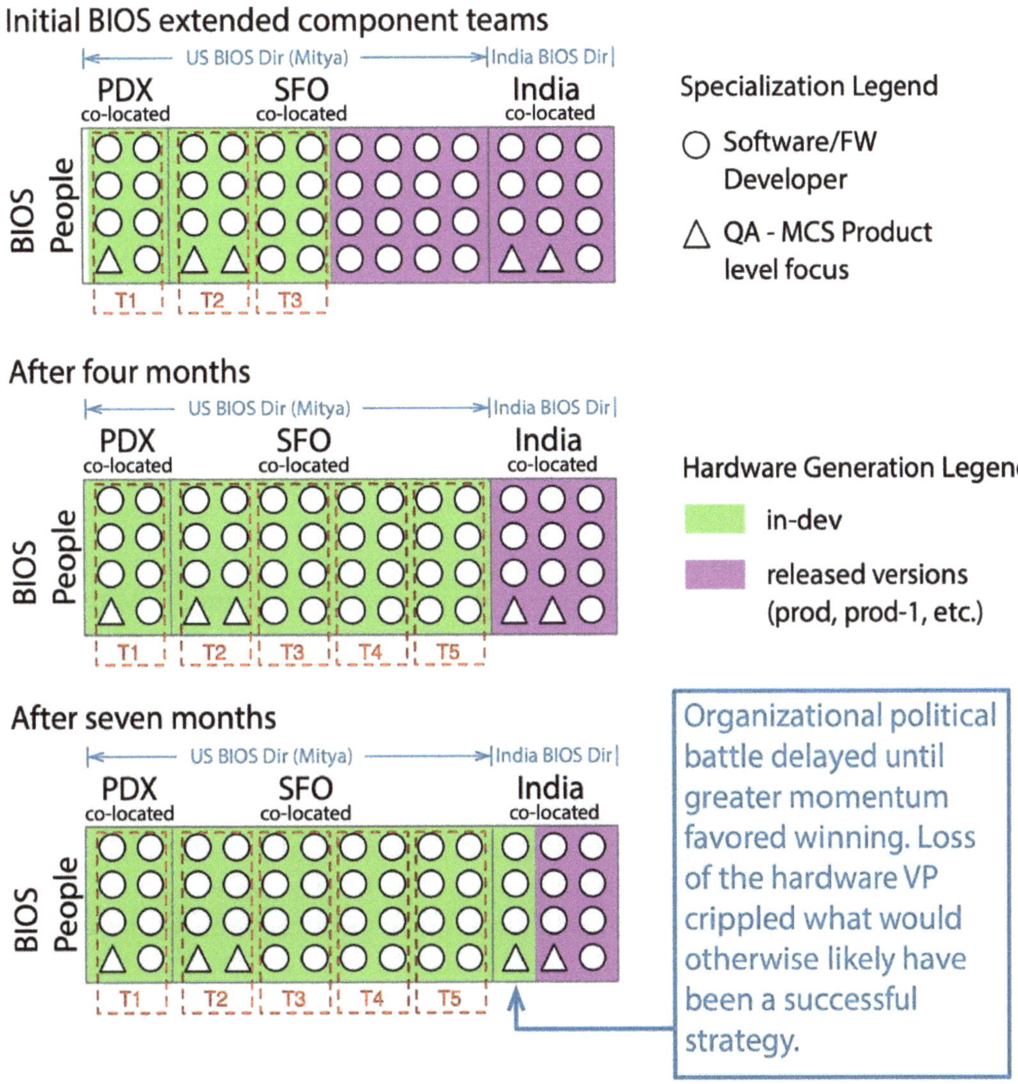

Figure 15: MCS hardware generation was used as one of the component dimensions in defining the boundaries of the LeSS-oriented adoption within the BIOS component. With the supportive hardware VP and a few trips to India it is likely Mitya and I would have been able to successfully work out the politics. Unfortunately, the change in the VP layer coupled with the layoffs precluded this strategy. The information in the timeline and organizational structure diagrams is relevant to what you see in this diagram.

Due to historical reasons the reality was that each new generation of hardware had an entirely separate BIOS code base with very little factoring of common functionality into reusable sub-components.

Interestingly this provided an opportunity to grow BIOS teams at a more sustainable pace. As previously uninvolved BIOS developers would finish working on escaped defects related to earlier production hardware generations, we would form additional cross-functional teams within the LeSS-oriented structure. The dynamics of the BIOS code base and the relationship with AMI will be explained in more detail further down.

This provided a half-year reprieve to establish cross-functional BIOS teams with US based people who reported through Mitya before needing to more actively involve the BIOS developers and managers in India. By the time the India BIOS engineers began to work on the same BIOS code base as the US based BIOS engineers, the US based BIOS engineers had jelled enough to push back when the India-based BIOS engineers not yet on a cross-functional BIOS team failed to meet the same improved quality standards.

Initial struggles were often as simple as ensuring India-based BIOS engineers were being careful not to check-in code unless it built cleanly and passed basic smoke tests. Additional automated testing along with a private CI server within the cross-functional BIOS teams' direct control helped the U.S.-based teams detect when problems were introduced by a developer not following the improved quality standards.

The success of the cross-functional BIOS teams ensured Mitya and I were in a much stronger political position to begin resolving the underlying structural issues. Mitya was delivering Nakashima-wide presentations on the improvements within the cross-functional BIOS teams at the behest of the Project Management SVP; so our success was definitely getting noticed.

The obvious solution for the India-based BIOS people was to on-board them as one or two additional cross-functional BIOS teams. Ideally all of these structural problems would have been solved from the very beginning, yet that had not been politically viable when we started. Instead, we did what was achievable. We intentionally creatively isolated and delayed the problem, while setting ourselves up for a future political win. We not only anticipated friction from two separate operating models, we were counting on it to make meaningful structural change politically achievable in the future.

Mitya and I were getting ready to travel to India and otherwise starting to work through the politics, about the time the supportive hardware VP resigned and the layoffs were announced. Had the hardware VP remained in place I think we would have been able to resolve the more pressing political challenges within the BIOS component boundary. We already had an India-based BIOS manager on our side, but we needed to work through some issues in the director layer.

Separate Codebases Not Good

Each new generation of hardware having an entirely separate BIOS code base was not a good thing. We used that fact to our advantage, yet it was far from desirable.

There was entirely too much copy-paste reuse, inadequate automated test coverage to enable developers to confidently make backward compatible changes, and a failure to use the AMI plugin layer to isolate any MCS related changes from AMI codebase changes.

This self-inflicted overburden made it far more difficult to adapt to changes in the Intel CPUs than would otherwise have been the case. Ironically, the *ability to adapt to changes* in Intel CPUs faster than Intel's release cycle is extremely critical to the MCS division's continuity of revenue and market share.

An effort to begin to resolve these issues can be seen in the *BIOS Definition of Done* section discussed later.

BIOS Geographically Dispersed Teams

From a perspective of optimizing for highest level adaptiveness in the service of learning and delivering highest-level value at a global level, there should never have been as many engineers working on the product as there were. The same could be said regarding the engineers being spread across multiple locations and timezones. Yet, that is where things started from, and trying to convince the organization otherwise from the beginning would not have been successful.

The criticality of being prepared for the Intel release date, coupled with the massive amount of copy-paste reuse in the legacy code base made for a challenging situation. Without the combined efforts of most of the US based BIOS team members there would not be enough combined knowledge to make the required changes in time, and to do so while concurrently addressing the poor engineering practices which caused the situation. In contrast, adding yet another region in a hugely different timezone just slowed things down.

A few different quotes from the LeSS books help highlight this point:

> Start with a small group of great people, and only grow when it really starts to hurt." That rarely happens. — ***Scaling Lean & Agile Development***
>
> Rather than debate if so many people are needed, we try to support people to improve their development with agile and lean principles so that at some point it becomes clear to the group that they have too many people in too many places. — ***Practices for Scaling Lean & Agile Development***

Quality Assurance Group Very Poorly Named

It is important to realize that quality can not be bolted on after the fact. Why? Product quality is the outcome of the entire product development system as a whole, not the responsibility of a separate quality control group. Although the formal title of the testing group was "Quality Assurance", a more accurate title would be "Quality Control".

A proper usage of quality assurance would refer to activities such as establishing test-first or test-driven development, establishing effective code review practices, putting static code analysis tooling in place, establishing continuous integration behaviors, and establishing pairing or swarming behaviors. Notice none of these practices have anything to do with trying to bolt on quality once the software development has been deemed "code-complete", or other nonsense.

The Quality Assurance group was indeed very poorly named. Even the very naming implies a broken mental model of how to best develop high-quality products. Yet, for the sake of historical accuracy I will continue to refer to the organizational branch which contained all the testers within the legacy structure as the QA group. Please remember this distinction when reading this document.

BIOS Testers Brought End-to-End Knowledge

The breadth and complexity of MCS coupled with a history of over-specialization, meant very few people understood the end-to-end product as well as the testers who had previously spent most of their time doing end-to-end testing in the legacy structure. Consequently, the testers brought just as much value to their respective BIOS teams as the traditional BIOS firmware developers.

The BIOS team members from a testing background still formally reported up through the Quality Assurance VP. Her support and that of the relevant QA Director was critical in enabling de facto equality within the BIOS teams. Retaining this formal reporting relationship was useful in obtaining the organizational acceptance of the radically improved quality being produced by the BIOS LeSS-oriented teams.

Retaining a separate reporting structure for the testers introduced a degree of systemic organizational fragility. A change in the Quality Assurance VP role could easily unravel much of the positive change that was happening. As a long-term goal, eliminating any formal testing specific distinction in the organizational structure would help avoid the risk of team members with a testing background being distracted by work unrelated to their team's Sprint Backlog.

Chapter 3 in *Practices for Scaling Lean & Agile Development* provides a comprehensive treatment of how to best approach testing at both a practical and strategic level.

Expanded BIOS Multi-Component Goals and Constraints

Although never formally documented outside of emails, whiteboard scribbles, and verbal conversations the goals of the BIOS LeSS adoption included:

- Improve the ability to adapt the MCS BIOS to any future changes in the MCS hardware, especially the routine periodic updates to the Intel chipsets.
- Create a culture which values technical excellence and avoids the unproductive stress created by the *Contract Game*.

BIOS support for the latest Intel chipset would seldom if ever be an important point of differentiation between the MCS product and that of its competitors, yet lack of parity during an Intel release event would drastically reduce market share and revenue overnight. This fact was well understood throughout the division's management. Consequently the following constraint was critical:

- The BIOS agile adoption efforts could never be allowed to be the reason the MCS product could not support a production version of an Intel CPU.

Consequently, although the BIOS adaptability goal was not at the forefront of senior management's mind to the extent it was in Mitya's, the importance of the goal was still implicitly well understood and valued.

Despite this shared understanding, the extent of the dysfunction with the traditional legacy waterfall approach was not widely accepted. The *Contract Game*, poor engineering practices, and over-specialization were observable throughout the division.

If you reflect on the goals above, you will find they resonate very strongly with both the LeSS perfection vision found in the *Organizational Perfection Vision* guide mentioned in *Large-Scale Scrum: More with LeSS.* You will also find they resonate strongly with the two questions in that guide for discerning a real system improvement from a local optimization.

Objectives within the BIOS group which supported the above goals included:

- Establish a single BIOS-component backlog, to make the highest-value BIOS work more visible. Baby steps towards a single product-level backlog.
- Expand the knowledge and skills of each engineer to encompass a broader portion of the product, thereby improving the adaptiveness of each team and the overall ability to switch to and then focus on newly-discovered highest-value work.
- Increased "whole product focus" (a LeSS principle) by each BIOS team while transitioning towards an expanded BIOS multi-component boundary spanning a greater portion of MCS.
- Work to improve the craftsmanship practices around the MCS BIOS component.
- Avoid the Contract Game as much as possible.

BIOS Adoption Story in Diagrams Alone

Taken together the timeline diagram, the component boundary diagrams, the feature adoption maps, organizational chart, and feature team expansion by hardware generation diagrams along with every diagram's respective caption provide a rather clear view of the overall story arch once you gain enough context to understand them.

BIOS Engineering and Cultural Challenges

Hopefully you now have a decent high level understanding of the role the customized BIOS system plays within MCS. While attempting to avoid going too deep into the details, I will try and summarize a few of the engineering and cultural challenges faced by the BIOS teams. Feel free to skip ahead if this is more detail than you care to bother with.

AMI provided foundation of BIOS code

The custom BIOS for MCS compute nodes had been created by modifying a constantly updated codebase licensed from AMI. Typical events driving AMI to make a continual stream of BIOS codebase changes include:

- Intel changes an aspect of the hardware to firmware interface in their prototype chipsets or reference board designs
- AMI adds support for this or that new BIOS functionality enabled by some improved features of the prototype Intel chipset or reference board designs
- AMI fixes a bug that AMI or one of the license partners identified
- AMI decides to change the BIOS codebase for any reason they believe makes sense

With largely stable interfaces between the MCS BIOS customizations and the AMI codebase, the impact of these normal AMI updates would be minimized. Alas that was seldom the case. Although some formal plug-ability existed with the AMI codebase, most of Nakashima's BIOS customizations had historically been made deep in the AMI codebase.

With each new chipset the MCS BIOS engineers would attempt to *copy* functionality from customizations used to adapt older BIOS versions to older chipsets into code for the new prototype chipsets. Similarly, the MCS BIOS engineers would attempt to keep current with any AMI code changes, merge those into their active working branch, and then manually retest. Some of the testing required hands-on work in the lab, although far more of the testing could have been automated than historically had been.

Death March Culture Driven by Intel Releases

The cadence of the market is dominated by Intel chipset release dates. Hardware integrators are given early access to prototype chipsets and reference board architectures. Ability to co-ship with Intel release dates is critical to staying viable within the market.

The intelligent organizational design decision would be to optimize for responsiveness to changes in Intel specifications. Unfortunately, the legacy organizational response had been to throw huge numbers of people at the problem and then death march towards a release date. Quality had inevitably been perpetually sacrificed on the altar of an impending release date.

Loss of Nakashima MCS Tribal Knowledge

Many of the people who initially built the constituent parts of Nakashima's MCS system left Nakashima over the years. As these people left, their tribal knowledge walked out the door with them. Ideally there would be extensive automated tests at all levels of the test pyramid and well crafted readable code. At a minimum there would at least be some useful documentation detailing the overall system architecture. As you would expect of any complex product developed under the delivery pressures of a waterfall culture, very little of any of this existed.

Intel BIOS is highly specialized

AMI estimates there are only somewhere on the order of a couple thousand engineers around the world who are familiar with BIOS customization. Many of the x86 hardware firmware interface behaviors and defacto specifications require tribal knowledge dating back to the early years of the PC revolution.

In practice, each area of customization in the MCS BIOS is the result of one or two engineers digging deep into the AMI code base and reverse engineering what they find there. In some ways this is no different than what any professional software engineer spends their day doing, the difference is just how esoteric and frequent this is within BIOS development.

Large number of engineers over three geographies

There was enough work to keep around forty engineers busy. With better craftsmanship practices it is likely far less people would eventually be needed. That said, it was going to take a tremendous amount of work and alignment just to dig out of all the self-inflicted technical problems.

Due to historical reasons, there were BIOS focused software, hardware, and test engineers spread across greater Portland, San Francisco, and Bengaluru. Any plan to scale the teams would have to solve the distributed problem. Fortunately, we were somewhat able to self-organize into co-located teams. Furthermore, the work being done by Bengaluru was somewhat independent of the efforts in Portland and San Francisco.

Largely Innate Technical Challenges

Although many of the challenges the MCS BIOS teams faced had been self-inflicted, some were largely inherent to the work itself. These included:

- Hardware updates to the prototype chipsets and boards would arrive periodically. The typical lead time for fabricating a new board design was around six weeks. One could argue some of this was less about the physics and more about organizational impediments.
- Prototype chipsets were just as likely to be responsible for problems as the firmware. Consequently, significant aspects of testing and troubleshooting required hands-on work in the lab.
- The x86 BIOS toolchain is extremely old and crufty as there was insufficient economic incentive for AMI to make significant investments improving the tooling.
- Software engineering practices such as automated unit testing are generally lacking within the entire world-wide x86 BIOS development culture. This cultural history was clearly observable within the AMI codebase, which the MCS BIOS teams customized. This created the following complications:
    - Any unit test tooling had to be entirely hand-rolled.
    - Wedging an effective dependency inversion mechanism into the AMI BIOS code base was much harder than it would have been in your typical Java or C# framework.

  - No books, articles, forum posts, example code, or other resources were available to provide unit test guidance in a BIOS context.
  - The concept of automated unit testing, yet alone test-first or TDD practices, was completely foreign to the MCS BIOS engineers.
- Everything in the world of low-level firmware development is more tedious than is typical of your average software development effort. A few examples relevant to the MCS BIOS include:
  - No operating system services exist because there is no operating system.
  - Code must be cross-compiled and then flashed to the target.
  - No TCP/IP network stack exists in early stages of the BIOS boot process, which makes it particularly difficult to communicate with the target early on. Early communication with the target device was limited to serial port communications and similar constrained mechanisms.
  - Most firmware development engineers tend to be people with greater microelectronics engineering expertise than software engineering expertise.

None of the problems listed here are insurmountable. In many cases techniques from other domains such as large web application development already provide insight into how to solve many of these problems.

For example, Java and C# both have sophisticated dependency injection frameworks available off-the-shelf. *Test Driven Development for Embedded C* by James Grenning is one example of an attempt to help improve cross-pollination of these techniques.

BIOS Adoption Efforts

Mitya Dubinksy and I realized the daunting scope of our endeavor. The steps we used to stand-up, launch, and mature the BIOS feature teams were largely the same as I had done with the diagnostics team. The main differences were in the level of difficulty and scale of the challenges involved.

The major differences mostly revolved around the rather straightforward scaling aspects.

BIOS Launch Steps

Mitya and I decided to initially focus on the engineers in San Francisco and Portland first. San Francisco and Portland were mostly focused on bringing up a new Intel chipset and board design. The engineers in Bengaluru were predominantly focused on fixing problems dealing with support for a chipset which was already in production.

I worked with Mitya to arrange training venues and to schedule Scrum training for every MCS BIOS engineer in San Francisco and Portland. We made sure to include a few closely collaborating test engineers from another group, and a few other relevant parties. If I remember correctly, this resulted in two training sessions in San Francisco and one in Portland over the course of three weeks. Mitya attended each training session in San Francisco. Mitya did not attend the Portland training, but Krishna Mishra was there providing support. Mitya did fly with me to Portland during the subsequent launch steps less than a week later.

The launch efforts were split across San Francisco and Portland. The initial two days of launch activity were conducted on a Thursday and Friday in San Francisco with the Portland BIOS team members conferenced in. The following week Mitya and I met up in Portland and continued the launch efforts with the Portland team members. This provided the Portland team members a better chance to influence, adjust, and ratify the work of the previous week. During the Portland launch efforts we frequently conferenced-in the San Francisco team members.

During the launch activity I wrote out a list of everything we needed to achieve, making sure everyone understood the intent of each item. I then largely took a back seat allowing the group to drive as much as possible, only stepping in when required. The list included things like creating an initial BIOS component backlog, figuring out a common Definition of Done, determining individual team boundaries, and working out event scheduling.

BIOS Component Backlog

The most interesting part of the launch effort revolved around the creation of the component backlog. The knowledge of what was needed to bring up the next Intel chipset was very broadly dispersed across the entire team. No one team member had a good understanding of the whole. The solution involved a couple days of brainstorming, followed by detailed refinement of individual PBIs in small working groups, and finally an incremental story mapping effort.

Initial Component Backlog Brainstorming

The structure of the initial BIOS component backlog brainstorming was fairly standard, the difference was the level of useful detail and alignment achieved and the amount of time required to do it well.

In this case the BIOS engineers were doing something they had collectively done many times before. As long as they collectively worked to pull the necessary knowledge out of each other's head, they were capable of creating a massive and detailed list of almost everything required. In retrospect I believe poor software practices such as copy-paste reuse and a reliance on manual testing meant the BIOS engineers had mostly been *re-tracing the same steps* with every new Intel chipset.

We would collaboratively write everything we could think of on post-it notes and place them onto the windows of a large corner conference room we had reserved. Mitya or another team member would then lead the group through each post-it. We gathered the post-it notes into sensible emergent groupings while concurrently consolidating duplicates. As the group discussed each post-it to gain consensus the participants would generate new post-its on the fly as it made sense. We would then spend a bit more time in small work groups generating new post-its before returning to a discussion session in which we consolidated everything again. This took us most of the first day. At the end of the first day we switched to some other items on the launch checklist, agreeing to let people prepare even more post-its for the next day.

On the morning of the second day we continued the BIOS Component Backlog brainstorming activity, concluding the brainstorming around lunchtime. We then went back to finishing up other things on the launch checklist.

We had enough Component Backlog to support the first Sprint, but not yet enough to achieve the level of useful detail we desired and knew was possible. If this were a new product being developed in a more typical software engineering context, I think what we did would be wasteful. Yet in this case, we were effectively consolidating and documenting years of tribal knowledge.

The *Initial PBR* guide in *Large-Scale Scrum: More with LeSS* covers *Initial Product Backlog Refinement* in more detail. One motivation includes:

> **Limited knowledge of customer-centric view**.
>
> Even if the old items were previously expressed in a customer-centric way, the prior siloed-specialists focus on narrow tasks, and so don't understand the full customer-centric view.

Chapter 5: Planning of *Practices for Scaling Lean & Agile Development* also has a variety of relevant experiments. The most directly relevant is *Try...Kickstart large-scale Scrum with one initial Product Backlog refinement workshop*.

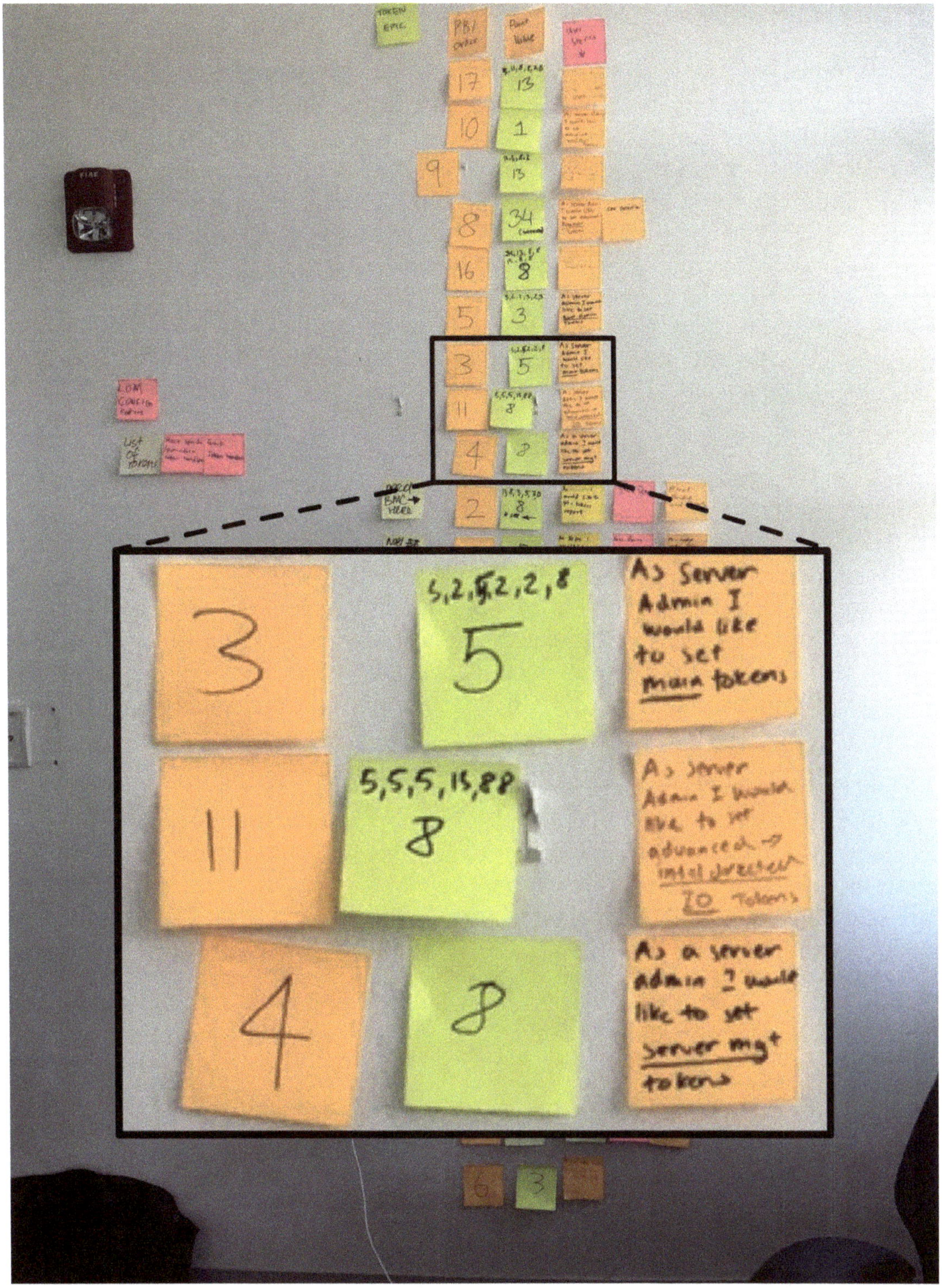

Figure 16: The initial BIOS component backlog brainstorming produced a series of preliminary PBI post-its with little more than short descriptions and/or titles. Each PBI post-it was assigned an effort estimate using poker planning, and given an appropriate order in the BIOS Component Backlog. Just before leaving we captured photos of our work in preparation for transitioning the data to electronic format.

Initial BIOS Component Backlog Refinement

Over the course of the first couple Sprints I worked with different small groups of engineers who knew the most about different aspects of the initial BIOS Component Backlog created during inception. I would remind each working group of the INVEST test, and help them work through the creation of a few PBIs. Once a group got a feel for what a well sliced PBI felt like, they would continue to work through every PBI they knew enough about to refine. In most cases I stayed with them to support them as they did this. It generally took each working group an hour or two to get a hang of how to turn a one-line description into a PBI with good acceptance criteria. It then took a working group another hour or two of effort to refine the remaining relevant higher priority PBIs into well refined PBIs. The developers in these working groups generally spanned two or more of the BIOS feature teams we formed during inception.

Once we felt we had enough detail in the BIOS Component Backlog, Mitya and I moved onto story mapping and affinity estimation. Mitya and I printed out the summary details of each PBI in small card format and started building out a story map in a small dedicated *information radiator* room near where the San Francisco BIOS teams sat. Mitya and I would pull in various groups of BIOS engineers anytime it made sense, while trying to be sensitive to any demands on their time. We eventually worked out a sensible BIOS Component Backlog ordering along with the MVP for the new Intel chipset and board design. The MVP turned out to be more than half of the component backlog. With all the complexity involved it took several sessions of an hour or two each over the course of several contemplative days before the story map started to settle down.

Towards the end of this initial refinement effort we called a larger meeting with every BIOS team member to review what we had on the wall. We used a combination of digital photos and video conferencing to enable the Portland team members to participate effectively. During this larger meeting the BIOS team members helped Mitya perform an overall sanity check of the story map. We also obtained rough effort estimates for every PBI within the MVP using affinity estimation.

Now that we had finally captured the collective knowledge of everyone on the BIOS teams, we settled into routine on-going refinement sessions which mostly focused on a shorter term horizon of a sprint or two out.

A variety of multi-site reference content from the LeSS books is listed in the Multi-Site Reference Content sub-section below.

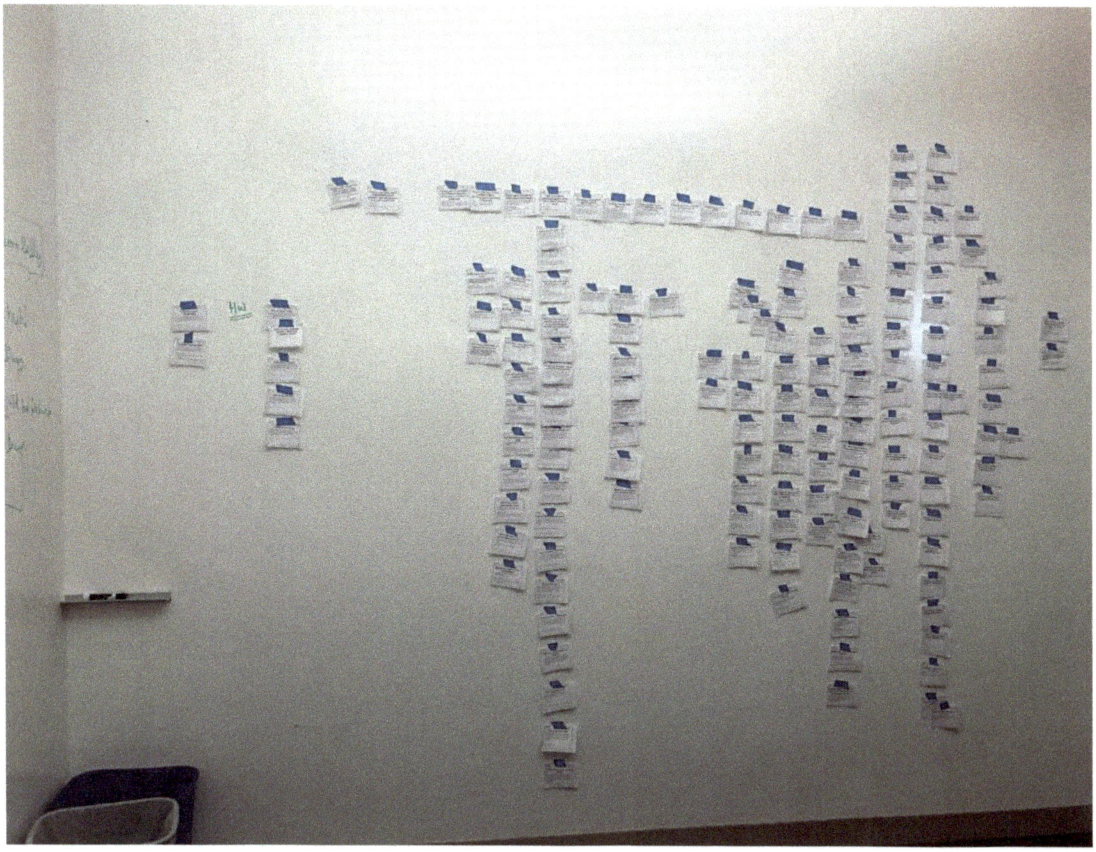

Figure 17: The brief post-it note PBIs from the initial two day launch meeting were further refined and stored electronically. These refinement efforts were done by small cross-team groups focused on particular areas of the BIOS component. It took a Sprint or more before the cross-team groups reached a point of diminishing return. Now that we had enough additional insight from the cross-team refinement efforts; we returned to a physical format to help us see the bigger picture. Here you see the story cards printed out and randomly taped to the wall in preparation for more refinement activities.

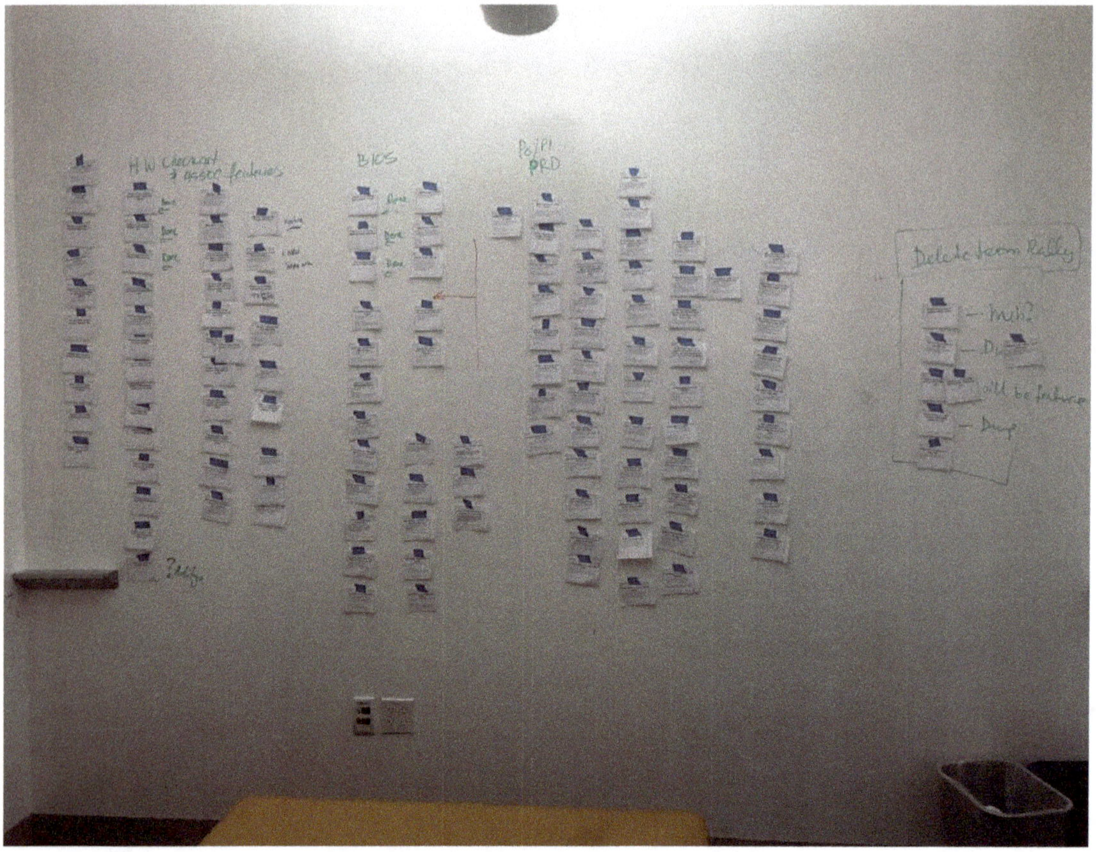

Figure 18: The BIOS Fake Product Owner began to look for natural groupings and orderings. The end result was a bit of a mix between a story map and a snake-like ordered Component Backlog with epic groupings. This large map was slowly evolved over the course of several days. Various groupings of people from the BIOS feature teams would be pulled in for more insight as it made sense. As the wall settled down the Fake Product Owner made sure to call a meeting with every BIOS Scrum team member to conduct an overall sanity check. At this point the MVP had become evident as seen by the red arrow.

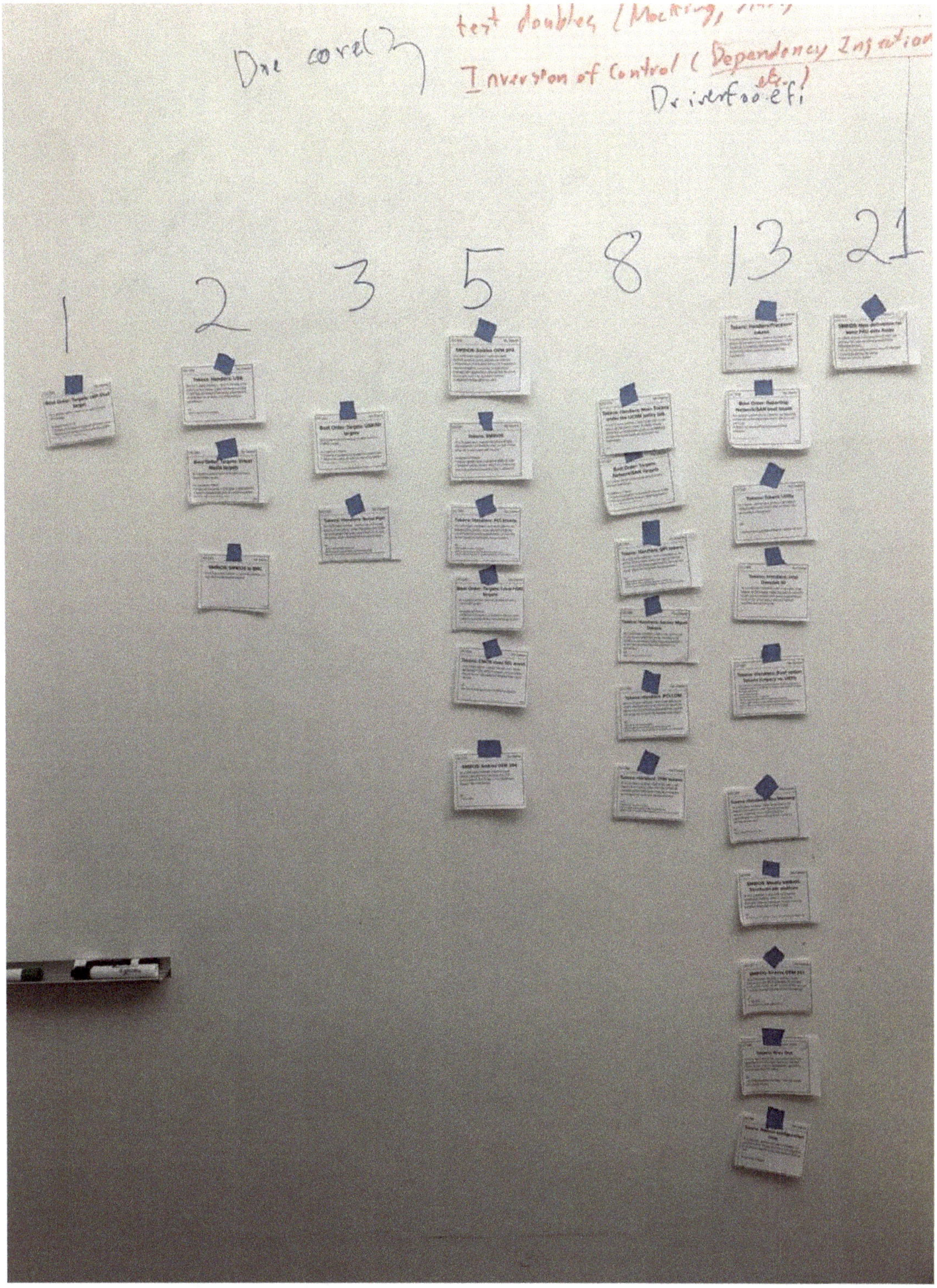

Figure 19: While every BIOS Scrum team member was available during the large group multi-team sanity check, affinity estimation was used to re-estimate every remaining PBI within the MVP. Afterwards the cards were rearranged into a cleaner story map version, and Rally was updated to reflect the new information.

Figure 20: Mitya ensured we had a helper to provide any masking tape we needed.

Multi-Site Reference Content

There is a great deal of useful content related to facilitating multi-site meetings in *Practices for Scaling Lean & Agile Development: Large, Multisite & Offshore Product Development with Large-Scale Scrum*. Even the sub-title implies as much.

Large-Scale Scrum: More with LeSS also includes a relevant narrative and a couple relevant guides.

Large-Scale Scrum: More with LeSS content includes:

- *Guide: Cross-Team Meetings*
- *Guide: Multi-Site PBR*
- *LeSS Huge Story: Multi-Site Teams*

Chapter 12: Multisite in *Practices for Scaling Lean & Agile Development: Large, Multisite & Offshore Product Development with Large-Scale Scrum* is entirely devoted to dealing with multi-site challenges. A few experiments within this chapter most directly related to the initial BIOS component backlog refinement effort include:

- Try...Seeing is believing—ubiquitous cheap video technology and video culture
- Try...Multisite planning poker (estimation poker)
- Try...Basic practices for multisite meetings

Reflecting on the Initial Refinement Efforts

The amount of detail and effort spent in refining the initial BIOS component backlog is certainly greater than any similar effort I have done before or since. Yet given the context I would do it again. We achieved a level of alignment, and enrollment of the BIOS engineers we would not have otherwise achieved.

The detail created is sure to be used in the future when extending the Component Backlog to account for future prototype Intel chipsets. With more use of the AMI plugin architecture the rework will be far less, so the details will vary. Yet the best place to start seeding new PBIs will be to look through what was done before.

We didn't so much force ourselves into some artificial set of refinement time-boxes. We determined what level of clarity and detail made the most sense in context, and then focused our energies to achieve it. Once done we switched gears and adopted cadenced cross-team refinement meetings.

BIOS Definition of Done

The second most interesting part of the inception effort was the Definition of Done creation. The team decided to ensure as much as possible they would move away from the terrible copy-paste behaviors of the past. They decided to be sure and leverage AMI's pluggable extension points whenever possible, and to pressure AMI to add any missing required extension points. You can see this commitment manifested in the more formalized Definition of Done included below. Look for the line starting with: "No changes outside of pluggable layer, ..."

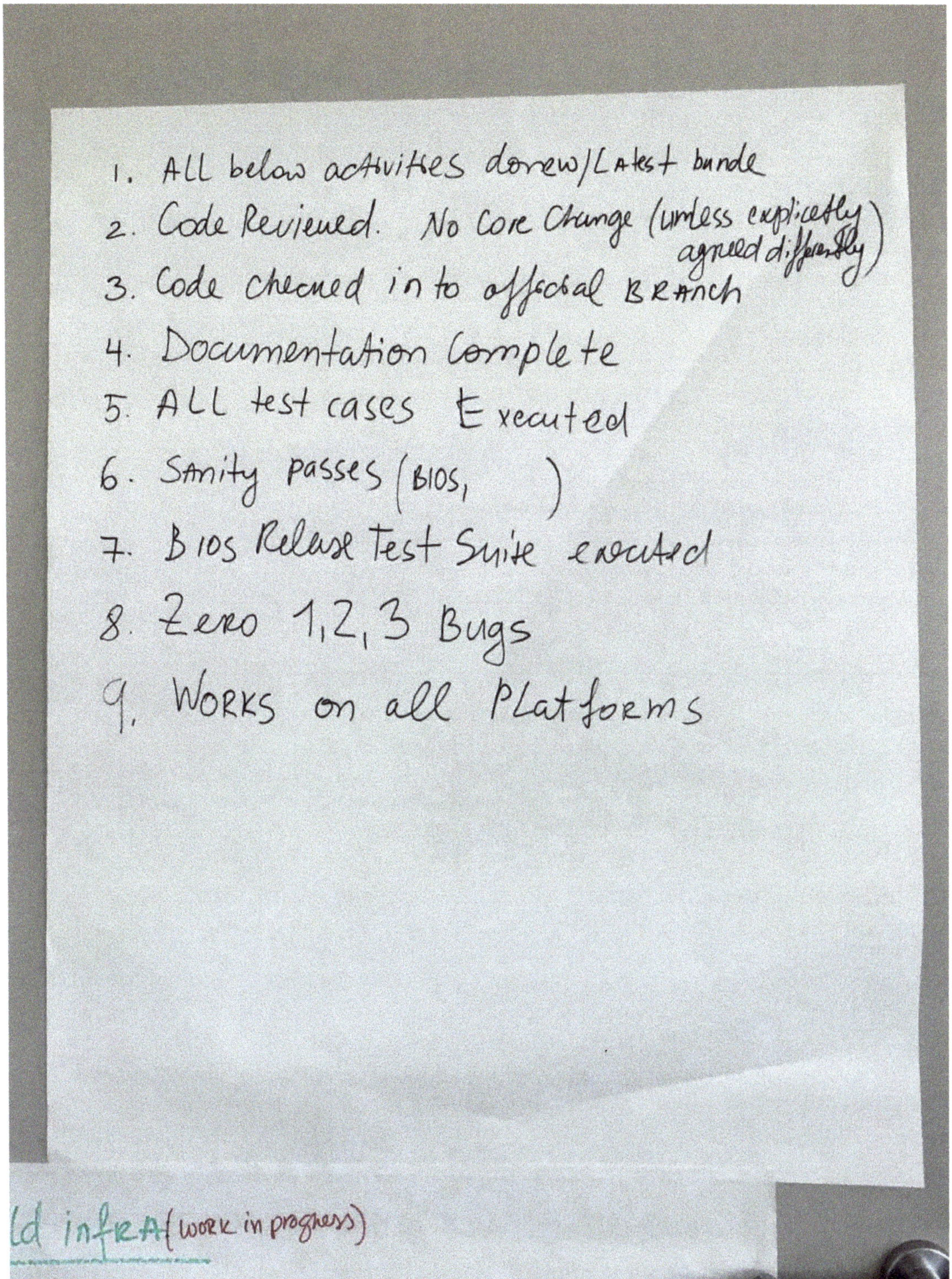

Figure 21: This is the initial draft Definition of Done created by the BIOS teams during their multi-day launch event.

Third Definition of Done (Firmware Component Teams in Waterfall Ecosystem)

Version: 1.23

Date: July 3, 2017

- ❑ All User Story acceptance criteria have been met.
- ❑ Relevant Epic acceptance criteria have been met.
- ❑ All activities below performed with latest third-party release bundle.
- ❑ Code peer reviewed in electronic peer review system.
- ❑ No changes outside of pluggable layer, unless agreed by third-party as an exception not handled by pluggable layer.
- ❑ Code checked into official branch.
- ❑ Documentation complete.
- ❑ Features documented via SW Spec Template and checked into document management system.
- ❑ All test cases executed (manual testing allowed).
- ❑ Test plan reviewed.
- ❑ Test management system used to track manual test cases.
- ❑ Zero defects in User Stories (within Dev Team control).
- ❑ Automated release test suite passes.
- ❑ Build is successful on all platforms and automated sanity test passes on all platforms.
- ❑ Legacy defects, or new defects from the waterfall side of the business follow the fire lane process.

Figure 22: The Definition of Done used by the BIOS teams evolved to what you see here after a few Sprints. This example Definition of Done along with additional context can be found in Table 9.3 of Forging Change.

BIOS Scrum Key Roles

Trent, Mitya, and I spent a great deal of thought trying to work out the best choice of Product Owner and Scrum Masters.

As I will explain in more detail, Mitya ended up being the only sensible choice of Product Owner available.

We also came to the conclusion I would initially need to act as the Scrum Master for all the teams. No other Scrum Master choice available had the necessary experience. Had we not been so reliant on having Mitya as the Product Owner, we would likely have selected Mitya as the Scrum Master.

More nuanced insight into our choices of Product Owner and Scrum Master is given below. Read if you have interest, and skip over if not.

Mitya as Temporary Fake Product Owner

Mitya was the director for all of the BIOS group. Mitya, Trent, and I recognized (and all Scrum experts recognize) it is usually hugely problematic for a Product Owner to have direct line authority over the members of the development team due to the imbalanced power relationship (see below). With another personality inhabiting the role this would likely have been a significant problem. In our case Mitya is such a naturally humble servant leader the conflict was not a significant issue.

Trent, Mitya, and I tried to figure out a better choice of Product Owner. In the end we realized there was no one else available who had enough component depth to be effective in the role while also having the right personality strengths. The other available candidates either had problematic personalities, or lacked sufficient knowledge of the overall MCS product and BIOS component to perform the role.

Avoid Line Manager as Product Owner

Just because we got away with Mitya as both the line manager and Fake Temporary Product Owner in our specific situation, I don't generally recommend you try the same. LeSS guidance on organizational structure explicitly avoids having team members report into the Product Owner.

The following quotes from *Large-Scale Scrum: More with LeSS* are instructive:

> **Peers, not peons**—If teams report to the Product Owner directly or indirectly in a hierarchical power relationship, that structure needs to change so that the teams and the Product Owner are peers collaborating. The Product Owner doesn't treat teams like peons for tasks, but fosters a collaborative relationship. — ***Guide: Five Relationships***
>
> An important point in this organizational structure is that the Teams and the Product Owner are *peers*—they do not have a hierarchical relationship. We have found it important to keep the power balanced between the roles. The Teams and Product Owner should have a *cooperative* peer relationship to together build the best possible product, and a peer structure supports this. This point is further explored in the Product Owner chapter. — ***Guide: LeSS Organizational Structure***

PO Concerns Arising from a Compromised Component Boundary

There were real Product Owner candidates in the product management group who we considered having as PO. Unfortunately, limits on the scope of influence of the relevant Vice President precluded expanding the component boundary far enough to result in a multi-component boundary any of these individuals had the domain knowledge to manage. It is important to remember even with an expanded BIOS multi-component boundary, the natural complexity of the MCS BIOS component as well as the overall MCS product is radically greater than the typical corporate information system.

Although we had buy-in from some of the most senior executives within the division, those executives had a multitude of other competing concerns to address. I'm fairly certain a few key divisional executives provided far more political air cover for our efforts than we will ever know. The ground level reality was it would take some time and more demonstrated success to gain enough political capital to make even more significant organizational changes on our behalf.

Until more of the highly specialized BIOS engineers were themselves more comfortable working across the various BIOS sub-components, an even broader expanded BIOS multi-component boundary would have stretched the technical and teaming capabilities of the BIOS teams more rapidly than was sustainable. Therefore further expanding the BIOS component boundary early on wasn't really an option anyway. These are the kinds of reasons that also motivate the LeSS guidance to *incrementally* expand a product definition, and to incrementally add Requirement Areas in a LeSS Huge adoption.

Relevant LeSS Product Rules

The following selected LeSS Framework rules are particularly relevant:

- There is one Product Owner and one Product Backlog for the complete shippable product.
- The Product Owner shouldn't work alone on Product Backlog refinement; she is supported by the multiple Teams working directly with customers/users and other stakeholders.
- All prioritization goes through the Product Owner, but clarification is as much as possible directly between the Teams and customer/users and other stakeholders.

Product Ownership Not The Biggest Challenge

From the perspective of the expanded BIOS multi-component, the customer problem is rather simple. The custom BIOS for each new Intel chipset has to provide the same services provided by previous generations of BIOS running on previous generations of Intel chipsets. Minor extensions of these capabilities are often required for each new chipset generation, yet they are minor in comparison to the base functionality. To some extent, the Fake Product Owner for BIOS was just an expert who worked with the teams to figure out a better way of solving the problems in the future.

The poor state of the code base was a consequence of historically poor engineering practices driven by the Contract Game. With constant pressure to meet unrealistic artificial "code-complete" deadlines imposed from the top, there had not been sufficient personal safety for craftsmanship. The history of massive amounts of copy-paste reuse coupled with poor automated test coverage provide two great examples of the self-inflicted wounds resulting from the Contract Game. The end result was to artificially make adapting the BIOS code base to each new generation of Intel chipset a monumental undertaking.

Ironically, with a more comprehensive Definition of Done and with a cross-functional team which could incrementally complete all the testing, there always had been sufficient time to do a better job. The Intel chipset release dates were real, but the waterfall stage gate dates were an artificial artifact arising from the imposition of a waterfall process.

The drastically improved quality being produced by the new BIOS teams would have changed this situation in time. Once the vast majority of the BIOS customizations were in a pluggable layer with better automated tests, it would likely become possible to adapt to a new Intel chipset with far less effort than in the past. Furthermore, with continued improvement efforts the BIOS teams would have fully expanded their capabilities to work all the way up through the MCS Admin layer.

Once both the quality improvements and the expansion of the component boundary had progressed far enough, the new teams would have both the available time and the skillset to handle far more dynamic requirements. Until that time, the truth is the expanded BIOS multi-component goals were so clear, and succinct -- and the work involved so massive -- there wasn't a lot of need for a Product Owner role. The truth is, this group of BIOS engineers with years of BIOS experience simply needed to charter a new path regarding how to better implement what they had already implemented many times before.

Once the BIOS teams had started to jell, the engineering practices had been improved, and the expanded BIOS multi-component boundary had been stretched up through the MCSA forming a natural Requirement Area of the overall MCS product, a real Product Owner from Product Management would eventually become critical.

Product Owner Selection Constraint Summary

All these reasons collectively brought us to selecting Mitya as the best mid-term choice for Product Owner. This is to say we chose to implement the *Fake Product Owner* experiment as described in *Practices for Scaling Lean and Agile Development* and the *Start Early or Messy with a Temporary Fake Product Owner* guide in *Large-Scale Scrum: More with LeSS.*

- The overspecialization and local focus of the BIOS teams, coupled with additional complexity introduced by years of poor engineering practices required having a Fake Product Owner to start. This person would have enough specialized technical depth to make sense of the BIOS Component Backlog and also maintain the respect of the BIOS teams.
- A Product Owner who by nature tended to empower others and avoided micromanagement was important in helping to establish a supportive context within which the BIOS teams could grow and mature.
- Since the BIOS LeSS-oriented structure was running inside of a large waterfall context still driven by the Contract Game, it was important to have a Product Owner who had enough positional and political influence to help establish a supportive context for the BIOS teams.
- Expanding the component boundary would help to reduce the BIOS specific knowledge necessary to understand and guide the BIOS component backlog and thereby enable other good choices of Product Owner. Until greater cross-functionality of the BIOS engineers made this possible, we would need a Fake Product Owner with a great deal of BIOS knowledge.
- The existence of a Fake Product Owner would further isolate the BIOS teams from the customers of the overall MCS product. We would look to move away from the need for a Fake Product Owner as soon as practical.

Coach as Scrum Master

There were not any full-time employees in the MCS division who we judged had enough experience to effectively guide the establishment of Scrum teams in as challenging a context as we were going to attempt with the BIOS teams. Any full-time employee selected would need to be gradually coached into the role.

Both Trent and I felt Mitya had the right personality, relationships, organizational knowledge, and component knowledge to be an excellent Scrum Master. Unfortunately, we really needed Mitya to take on the Product Owner role until the component boundary could be further expanded.

We ultimately decided I would initially need to act as the Scrum Master. Trent and I were careful to ensure I had the bandwidth available to perform the role. I moved into an empty desk in the BIOS engineering area and spent the next several months largely devoted to launching and maturing the BIOS teams. Since I flew in every week anyway, I could travel to Portland whenever it made sense. As a practical matter Mitya and I did most things together. I would continually help Mitya and other strong natural leaders in the group grow into leading most activities themselves.

As the BIOS teams gelled and began to mature a couple of additional natural Scrum Master candidates emerged. These were not necessarily engaged with Scrum to begin with, yet they became so over time. Mitya and I focused on growing these particular individuals into potential future Scrum Masters as we identified them.

The following recommendation from Mitya illuminates the challenging context involved:

> Working with James was a transformational experience for me, and for the team.
>
> He took us from "No Way Scrum Can Be Done Here" to "We Can't Ever Go Back". He brought the team from Waterfall to Scrum.
>
> We are a team of Firmware engineers and firmly believed that Scrum does not belong in our field. James demonstrated that Scrum is a framework to bring focus to the Software Craftsmanship, Quality, and way of planning our work.
>
> James coached me to act as a Product Owner, and coached the team past the learning curve of the Scrum framework.
>
> The team found extremely useful his focus on the technical aspect of development, test, CI/CD. He introduced a number of concepts and tools to us, and worked with team members on the technical side where it was needed.
>
> Results are very straightforward. We have been practicing Scrum for almost a year. We have much better visibility into the backlog. The team engagement is better. The initial product quality is better.

Scrum Master Selection Constraint Summary

- The exotic hardware and firmware engineering context coupled with the cultural challenges involved were too challenging for the skill-set of any full-time Scrum Master candidate available.
- Mitya had the natural aptitude to be quickly grown into an effective Scrum Master. This option was precluded due to our need for Mitya to act as the Fake Product Owner.
- Once it became politically and technically practical to expand the component boundary we could replace Mitya as Product Owner, transitioning Mitya or anyone else who showed promise and growth to a Scrum Master role.
- I was the only person available to us with a strong enough Scrum Master skill-set to attempt such a challenging Scrum adoption. I could only do it by leaning heavily on the BIOS developers, Mitya, and others for guidance as we collectively found our way to improving things.

BIOS Teams Self-Selected

During inception we collaboratively worked out who would be on each new team.

Having the Portland people form a single team was an easy decision for the group. There were only a half dozen or so people in Portland. This included software, hardware and test engineers. Mitya, Krishna, Trent, and I had worked to ensure this would be the case way back when we decided who we would train in Portland. I think Krishna may have helped us find an appropriate test engineer we took from a group working on another part of MCS.

The real challenge was who would be on which of the San Francisco teams, and how many San Francisco teams there would be. We initially ended up with two. As I recall the group made an initial pass at self-designing their team compositions on the afternoon of the first launch day. After some contemplation and thought overnight, the group made a few minor adjustments to the team compositions on the second day of the launch.

In a few months we would roll in a few more developers working on the edges of the BIOS component boundary and form another team or two working within the same LeSS-oriented structure.

Although the Portland team was largely co-located, there were initially a few critical engineering skills they were missing. For a little while one or two San Francisco engineers were members of the Portland team. Over time I believe the Portland engineers became entirely self-sufficient.

BIOS Cadence and Sprint Timing

The group decided on a two week cadence. We made sure the Sprint boundary was mid-week so that I could be available to the teams and not somewhere in the stratosphere sitting on a plane.

BIOS Retrospective Structure Adaptation

We tried several variations on a combination of cross-team and per-team retrospectives. The retrospective structure was similar in spirit to the LeSS Sprint Rules, although it varied slightly in the details.

From a retrospective meta-structure perspective we typically followed the advice seen in *Agile Retrospectives* by Esther Derby and Diana Larsen. The most common techniques were simple brainstorming with dot voting, time-boxed discussions, and the use of a brief four-box retrospective on the retrospective structure itself.

Initial Retrospective Structure

The initial retrospective structure was as follows:

1. Cross-team meeting to identify the highest priority cross-team discussion item
2. Per-team retrospectives to discuss per team issues as well as the highest priority cross-team item
3. Cross-team meeting (a LeSS Overall Retrospective) to discuss the output of the per-team meetings and to come to consensus on an approach to solving the cross-team issue

Both cross-team meetings included all team members from every BIOS team, Mitya (the Fake Product Owner), and myself (acting Scrum Master).

The first cross-team meeting was focused on identifying any cross-team team issue the group felt was important for the team level retrospectives to consider. The intent was to provide an opportunity for people to work out potential solutions to the cross-team issue in smaller team level discussions, such that the subsequent cross-team meeting would benefit from deeper insights that might not have surfaced in a larger group discussion.

You will notice this is very similar to the LeSS Framework structure of team level retrospectives followed by an overall retrospective. The key difference is the team level retrospectives were sandwiched between the first and second part of an overall retrospective.

In practice, the team level retrospectives seemed to spend most of their time on whatever issues were identified in the first part of the overall retrospective. Had the team level retrospectives been conducted before any overall retrospective meeting as the LeSS framework prescribes I believe the team level retrospectives may have been more insightful.

Most of the problems surfaced were cross-team in nature. I don't know if this was simply a result of context, or whether having a portion of the overall retrospective before the team level retrospectives had the effect of unintentionally distracting the teams from more challenging team level discussions.

Later Retrospective Structure

We were generally careful to close the final cross-team retrospective with a retrospective on the retrospective itself. From this we eventually decided to change to the following retrospective structure.

1. Cross-team meeting to identify the highest priority cross-team discussion items
2. Breakout groups for the top few dot voted issues. Break-out groups tended to cross team boundaries, with people often self-selecting to attend the breakout they were most passionate about or most needed for.
3. Cross-team meeting to discuss output of breakout group meetings and to come to consensus on an approach to solving the cross-team issues discussed

As you can see this structure was identical to the initial structure with the exception of the middle step. Rather than breaking into per-tegam retrospectives we were breaking off into working groups which cut across team boundaries, and aligned with whatever people felt most they had the most affinity with.

In practice the Portland team generally stayed as a team during the second step. We generally conducted any cross-team events in a set of tele-presence rooms. If anyone in San Francisco felt particularly passionate about the topic the majority of the Portland folks had taken, we would use the tele-presence room for that topic. Other working groups would go elsewhere in other break out rooms with limited tele-presence capability.

How the retrospective working groups split up in San Francisco was often somewhat random. We would often split down the middle of a conference table, with a few people switching working groups when it made sense.

Given the naturally collaborative nature and relationship history of the people involved, lack of a dedicated per-team retrospective didn't seem to matter. In other groups I have worked with, per-team retrospectives often turn out to be crucial. Perhaps with time and additional teams the dynamics would have shifted such that the group would have decided to restore team level retrospectives.

Larger Structural Issues Not Addressed in Overall Retrospectives

In LeSS, the overall retrospective is intended to address broader systemic issues. Although the BIOS teams actively addressed and implemented solutions to cross-team systemic issues within their control, there was little ability to address broader systemic issues. Neither the VP layer managers, nor the new SVP manager ever attended.

See *Guide: Overall Retrospective* in *Large-Scale Scrum: More with LeSS* for more nuance around this topic.

BIOS Alignment to LeSS Rules

Before going on to discuss a few more details and insights from the BIOS teams, it is instructive to review alignment to the formal LeSS Rules.

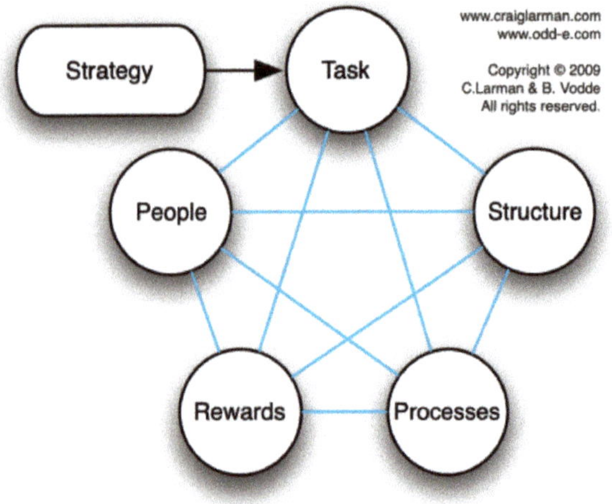

Figure 23: In Scaling Lean and Agile Development, Larman and Vodde talk about organizational strategy in terms of Jay Gilbrith's star model. Some of the greatest problems in the LeSS adoption relate to Rewards and People, and their intersection with Structure. There was a failure to flatten the formal organizational structure, coupled with insufficient attention to compensation structures which reward technical proficiency at the same level as managerial proficiency. It is useful to keep Gilbrith's model in mind as you read through the BIOS Alignment to LeSS Rules section. (Figure used with permission).

LeSS Structure Alignment

- Structure the organization using real teams as the basic organizational building block.

  Yes

- Each team is (1) self-managing, (2) cross-functional, (3) co-located, and (4) long-lived.

  self-managing: Every team was self-managing from day one. The teams controlled how much work they pulled into a Sprint, collaboratively tasked out each Sprint, had full control of their architectural decisions within the BIOS codebase, ran their own daily scrums, and everything else one might expect of a self-managing team.

  cross-functional: Early on each team tended to have a strong affinity for certain areas of the BIOS component. Growing into being more cross-functional even within the BIOS component took each team a while. As teams further evolved they began to progressively stretch themselves outside of their original affinities.

The existence of a common BIOS Component Backlog and single Fake Product Owner created structural forces which continually encouraged increasing levels of cross-training within and across teams.

As the BIOS teams worked to further stretch the BIOS component boundary up through the MCSA the teams slowly became further cross-functional from an overall MCS product perspective. This never reached its full potential, yet one team with an affinity for MCSA related BIOS work was certainly on that path. This topic will be explored further in the *BIOS Component Boundary Expanded* section.

co-located: Each team was mostly co-located. Since the Portland team lacked knowledge in a few areas of the BIOS codebase, the Portland team initially had one or two members based in the San Francisco area. The teams worked to aggressively do the cross-training to resolve these exception cases. As I recall the San Francisco team based members of the Portland team were able to leave the Portland team and join one of the San Francisco teams within a few sprints.

long-lived: The teams largely stayed intact for months on end. The massive layoffs obviously eventually impacted the longevity. There was also a bit of self-directed shuffling of members across teams as the Portland team became less dispersed and as more BIOS developers became available for working on the in-development hardware generation of BIOS. Generally speaking the newly available team members formed up new teams, with the original three teams remaining fairly stable.

So the teams were not ultimately as long-lived as I would have liked, yet they certainly were not being randomly retasked to new teams every few months.

When looking at longevity from a multi-year timescale, there was definitely a problem. In *Scaling Lean and Agile Development*, Larman and Vodde talk about organizational strategy in terms of Jay Gilbrith's star model. Of the various elements, the Rewards and People elements were not given sufficient attention.

Although the pre-existing compensation structure already provided some level of incentive for engineers to continue on a technical track, the financial and cultural incentives for moving up the managerial ladder remained much stronger. Similarly, the continual pressure cooker resulting from the commitment game being played at the highest levels of the division left little time for significant learning and professional growth.

- The majority of the teams are customer-focused feature teams.

Although the teams were largely vertically sliced within the BIOS component boundary, the BIOS component boundary was itself a compromise. As the BIOS teams matured we worked to establish an even more vertical expanded multi-component boundary slicing through the entirety of the MCS product, although never as vertical as we might have eventually achieved.

- Scrum Masters are responsible for a well-working LeSS adoption. Their focus is towards the Teams, Product Owner, organization, and development practices.

  Yes

- A Scrum Master does not focus on just one team but on the overall organizational system.

  Yes

- A Scrum Master is a dedicated full-time role.

  Yes

- One Scrum Master can serve 1-3 teams.

  I was serving 5 teams by the time all of the US based BIOS engineers had been rolled into feature teams. In practice I shared much of the load with Mitya and others we were growing into Scrum Masters.

- In LeSS, managers are optional, but if managers do exist their role is likely to change. Their focus shifts from managing the day-to-day product work to improving the value-delivering capability of the product development system.

  Yes. Mitya, Trent and I kept the effective structure very flat. I don't recall Mitya ever focusing on managing the day-to-day BIOS component work.

- Managers' role is to improve the product development system by practicing Go See, encouraging Stop & Fix, and "experiments over conformance."

  Yes.

  Mitya and I were both sitting with the SFO based teams and would also fly to Portland from time to time. Various examples of Go See and experiments over conformance include:

  - Both Mitya and I would occasionally pair program with one or more BIOS developers and/or attend design discussions when deemed beneficial.
  - Mitya and I would actively meet with various people up, down, and across the organization to help work through numerous organizational impediments.
  - I spent significant time pairing with Emmett Brown as we worked out how to create automated unit tests for BIOS code.
  - I spent significant time pairing with a couple developers to stand up a CI server within the BIOS team's control.
  - BIOS team retrospectives consistently identified at least one experiment every Sprint which the teams took action on in the respective subsequent Sprint.

- For the product group, establish the complete LeSS structure "at the start"; this is vital for a LeSS adoption.

  Yes, within the scope of the extended BIOS component. No, within the broader overall MCS product scope.

- For the larger organization beyond the product group, adopt LeSS evolutionarily using Go and See to create an organization where experimentation and improvement is the norm.

  Yes

LeSS Product Alignment

- There is one Product Owner and one Product Backlog for the complete shippable product.

  Yes for the BIOS component. No for the overall MCS product.

- The Product Owner shouldn't work alone on Product Backlog refinement; she is supported by the multiple Teams working directly with customers/users and other stakeholders.

  Yes

- All prioritization goes through the Product Owner, but clarification is as much as possible directly between the Teams and customer/users and other stakeholders.

  Yes for the BIOS component. No for the overall MCS product.

- The definition of product should be as broad and end-user/customer centric as is practical. Over time, the definition of product might expand. Broader definitions are preferred.

  Yes in terms of expanding the BIOS component boundary as broadly as possible. No in terms of the lack of a LeSS context encompassing the entire MCS product.

- One Definition of Done for the whole product common for all teams. Each team can have their own stronger Definition of Done by expanding the common one.

  Yes in terms of the common Definition of Done used by the BIOS teams. No in terms of the overall MCS product.

- The perfection goal is to improve the Definition of Done so that it results in a shippable product each Sprint (or even more frequently).

  Yes in terms of the BIOS component. There was a little bit of Undone work we couldn't avoid until we could extend the LeSS adoption more broadly over the entire MCS product..

LeSS Sprint Alignment

- There is one product-level Sprint, not a different Sprint for each Team.

  Yes in terms of the BIOS extended component teams.

- Each Team starts and ends the Sprint at the same time. Each Sprint results in an integrated whole product.

  Yes in terms of the BIOS extended component teams.

- Sprint Planning consists of two parts: Sprint Planning One is common for all teams while Sprint Planning Two is usually done separately for each team. Do multi-team Sprint Planning Two in a shared space for closely related items.

  Yes in terms of the BIOS extended component teams.

- Sprint Planning One is attended by the Product Owner and Teams or Team representatives. They together tentatively select the items that each team will work on that Sprint. The Teams identify opportunities to work together and final questions are clarified.

  Yes in terms of the BIOS extended component teams.

- Each Team has their own Sprint Backlog.

  Yes in terms of the BIOS extended component teams.

- Sprint Planning Two is for Teams to decide how they will do the selected items. This usually involves design and the creation of their Sprint Backlogs.

  Yes in terms of the BIOS extended component teams.

- Each Team has their own Daily Scrum.

  Yes in terms of the BIOS extended component teams.

- Cross-team coordination is decided by the teams. Prefer decentralized and informal coordination over centralized coordination. Emphasize Just Talk and informal networks via communicate in code, cross-team meetings, component mentors, travelers, scouts, and open spaces.

  Yes in terms of the BIOS extended component teams.

- Product Backlog Refinement (PBR) is preferably done with multiple teams to increase shared learning and to exploit coordination opportunities.

  Yes in terms of the BIOS extended component teams.

- There is one product Sprint Review; it is common for all teams. Ensure that suitable stakeholders join to contribute the information needed for effective inspection and adaptation.

  Yes in terms of the BIOS extended component teams.

- Each Team has their own Sprint Retrospective.

  Initially yes in terms of the BIOS extended component teams. We later deviated a bit as described earlier in the *BIOS Retrospective Structure Adaptation* section.

- An Overall Retrospective is held after the Team Retrospectives to discuss cross-team and system-wide issues, and create improvement experiments. This is attended by Product Owner, Scrum Masters, Team representatives, and managers (if any).

  Yes in terms of the BIOS extended component teams.

BIOS Triage Rules

The BIOS teams were often distracted by demands from engineers and management working on other parts of the overall MCS system. Some of these demands required prompt action in service of the overall MCS development efforts, while other demands were best promptly rejected or perhaps moved into and prioritized within the BIOS Component Backlog.

With the exception of a few test engineers, all the BIOS Scrum development team members reported directly into Mitya. The problem of functional managers distracting BIOS team members who reported to them was largely non-existent.

The distractions were predominately a function of the imperfect BIOS component boundary when compared to the actual MCS product boundary, and the over coupling of the MCS BIOS code with the AMI BIOS code.

Creating a formalized set of triage guidelines was very helpful in managing these distractions until the underlying root causes could be more fully addressed. Benefits included:

- Respecting the Product Owner's intent
- Remaining responsive to critical unanticipated demands
- Helping BIOS engineers say no to inappropriate demands
- Providing transparency to everyone involved
- Consolidating the collective wisdom of the BIOS engineers
- Achieving alignment within the BIOS teams
- Ability of the BIOS Scrum teams better inspect and adapt based on historical data

Example Triage Guidelines
Version: 0.33
Date: July 4, 2017

Add to the **Sprint Backlog**, and start work immediately if:

- ❑ I see an email from partner company regarding future platform with subject [Blah-blah] or [Blah-RC]
- ❑ I see an email from build system team, build is broken
- ❑ I see an email indicating the automated long-duration system test failed
- ❑ I see an email from the partner company with Future Platform label notification
- ❑ Platform team believes delaying the work will affect hardware schedule
- ❑ The issue is known to be blocking manufacturing

Add to the **Sprint Backlog**, and start work after approval (PO will likely say yes) if:

- ❑ I get an email from partner company regarding a shipping platform with the subject [Blah-blah] or [Blah-RC] and I then convince myself this is a critical release that needs immediate attention and cannot wait until the next Sprint
- ❑ Severity 1 or Severity 2 bug
- ❑ Issue is raised by manufacturing, but not a blocking item
- ❑ Issue is raised by HW/[Sub-System X]/[Sub-System Y]/[Sub-System Z] teams, but not a blocking item

Add to the **Product Backlog**, we'll prioritize during Product Backlog refinement meetings if:

- ❑ I get an email from partner company with Shipping Platform label notification
- ❑ I get an email with "+Bob" without clear indication of urgency
- ❑ Someone says: "Hi, we need Sam or Sally's help with …"
- ❑ New Severity 3 or lower bug is reported.
- ❑ Asked to work on old Severity 3 or lower bug
- ❑ Platform issue reported, but is not bound to an immediate date

Figure 24: This triage guideline used by the BIOS teams establishes three basic categories: take immediate action, ask the Product Owner, and put it on the BIOS Component Backlog. The Product Owner has clearly communicated intent while empowering the Scrum Development Teams to take immediate action when appropriate. By making the guidelines explicit, the Product Owner also improves the odds of collaboratively refining the guidelines based on the collective wisdom of the teams.

BIOS Unit Testing Is Possible

Where there is a will, there is a way. We knew automated unit testing within BIOS was going to be extremely challenging. No TCP/IP network stack existed during early stages of development, very few of the standard C library functions are available, all code has to be cross-compiled and flashed to the target, and no existing approach to unit testing within the AMI BIOS ecosystem could be found.

Although I spent well over a decade as a software engineer practicing test first development, I know almost nothing about BIOS and low level hardware design. Similarly, the BIOS engineers had almost no exposure to the languages, tooling, design patterns, and various craftsmanship practices seen in higher performing middle-ware teams. In many ways most of the MCS BIOS engineers are electronic engineering wizards with very narrow software engineering skills.

Emmett Brown was a passionate engineer who was determined to figure out how to move towards test first development for the MCS BIOS code. I worked with Emmett to help him understand the design elements required, and to show him examples of each in various higher level development ecosystems. Emmett would in turn teach me about various details of the UEFI standard, the BIOS tool-chain, and the hardware constraints involved. We would then puzzle through the challenges and consider different approaches to solving the problem.

It took a few weeks of work, but Emmett eventually had a working prototype in place. He used part of the UEFI standard to achieve dependency inversion, hand coded his test doubles, ported a crude C unit test framework, and built a basic transport protocol over a serial connection to get the results back to the Windows workstation or CI server which had the build toolchain orchestrating the effort.

I have heard engineers in far less technically challenging contexts developing in an imperative language provide all kinds of reasons as to why automated unit testing isn't technically possible. Don't believe them. Emmett achieved automated unit testing working way down in the primordial ooze of a complex half-instantiated circuit board in a context without any useful pre-built unit test tooling.

BIOS Team Count Increases

In order to keep the initial adoption scope manageable only those working on support for the newest Intel chipset and reference board design were originally included. Anyone working on bug fixes and other minor work related to the older production Intel chipsets continued to work within the legacy organizational design. Said another way, the BIOS component boundary only included the newest prototype Intel chipset.

Since each major Intel release involved a separate AMI codebase, this strategy worked fairly well. By the time the work related to the legacy Intel chipsets tapered off, the first three BIOS Scrum teams had largely jelled.

As additional San Francisco BIOS developers became available, and so we formed two new teams working off of the single combined BIOS Component Backlog. Each new team was allowed to influence and ratify the various cross-team artifacts to help ensure their full engagement and commitment to the process. I don't recall, but I'm sure I ran anyone who still needed it through agile overview training as part of this effort.

As we rolled in the two new BIOS Scrum teams, we effectively expanded the BIOS component boundary at the same time to include all generations of the Intel chipset.

BIOS Component Boundary Expanded

At the top of the MCS system is the Modular Compute System Administrator (MCSA) which is responsible for administering the entirety of the MCS infrastructure. When the system administrator at a customer of MCS interacts with MCS, it is typically the MCSA they are interacting with.

Some of the enhancements in the MCS BIOS code required making small changes in the MCSA. Less commonly changes would also have to be made within the firmware running on a low power node controller running on each node.

Initially the BIOS teams would collaborate with a few of the more senior MCSA developers for any cross-cutting functionality. The BIOS Scrum teams often found coordinating their work with the MCSA developers challenging. The MCSA developers were suffering under all the normal delivery pressures inherent in a waterfall managed project.

Had it been politically viable to start with a broader expanded BIOS component boundary which aligned with a natural Requirement Area of the overall MCS product to begin with none of the coordination issues above would have existed.

In consideration of the political situation the obvious solution was for the MCS BIOS developers to slowly develop the expertise to make MCSA changes themselves. As the BIOS Scrum teams matured, this need became increasingly obvious to many of the BIOS Scrum teams. I also tended to encourage them in this direction.

Through a variety of conversations we were able to get buy-in from a small handful of engineers who worked within MCSA, and from another set who worked within the node controller firmware. The agreement was to have them help guide the BIOS Scrum teams in identifying when a cross-cutting change would be simple enough the BIOS Scrum could make the change themselves. The BIOS Scrum team would then do the work and have the relevant expert outside the BIOS team perform code review.

The San Francisco BIOS developers had been successfully collaborating with many of the San Francisco MCSA developers for years. From the perspective of the key MCSA team leads and architects, anything the BIOS teams could do to take care of some of the MCSA/BIOS integration work was seen as a welcome reprieve. So the fact the Software VP was passively aggressively working to maintain the status quo turned out not to be a significant issue in practice. As long as the MCSA/BIOS integration work got done, no one in senior management cared how it happened.

The Node Controller developers reported up through the same director who had been involved in helping to establish the diagnostic team. So there were no significant political challenges dealing with cross-training the BIOS teams to make small changes within the Node Controller. Most of the Node Controller developers sat in the same small Portland office the Portland BIOS team did.

Mitya and I reasoned the success of this approach would grow over time. We predicted it would eventually become politically difficult not to reassign one or two MCSA experts to the BIOS group. The more the BIOS Scrum teams gained the ability to work end to end across MCS, the more natural the BIOS component boundary would become. More and more of the Product Backlog Items would become something meaningful to the MCS product management group. As that happened Mitya could transition out of being the Fake Product Owner. He could then work to further improve team dynamics and help grow effective Scrum Masters to take my place.

But before significant action could be taken on the agreement to start stretching at least one BIOS team outside of the BIOS code base, the division began to erode around us. *The Support System Collapses* section farther down will elaborate a bit more on the senior management changes and layoffs.

BIOS India Team Challenges

The tremendous time zone differences between the San Francisco and India offices were always a challenge. Similarly, the different reporting lines also tended to complicate alignment issues. A few of the complexities are detailed below.

It is instructive to reflect upon the following LeSS Framework and LeSS Huge Framework rules:

- *For the product group, establish the complete LeSS structure "at the start"; this is vital for a LeSS adoption.*
- *LeSS Huge adoptions, including the structural changes, are done with an evolutionary incremental approach.*

With broader senior level management buy-in some of the challenges encountered in working with the India teams could have been structurally addressed earlier on. On the other hand only so much change at any one time would have been sustainable. It is important to remember the actively enrolled original engineering SVP had left by the time the BIOS LeSS adoption was launched.

Throughout the BIOS agile adoption, Mitya and I made sure to broadly socialize the work we were doing. Even engineers working on the legacy support for older Intel chipsets were aware of the Definition of Done being used for the new Intel chipsets. Lead engineers from India often dialed-in from their home to attend the LeSS-oriented Sprint Reviews.

In Figure 15 and the nearby *BIOS Organizational Context* section I described the tactic Mitya and I took of isolating and delaying the organizational changes for the India-based BIOS developers. The ability to use the Intel chipset generation as one of the expanded multi-component boundaries and the fact India was initially focused on fixing problems related to older generations of the Intel chipset is what made this possible. This was a risky strategy in that it depended upon continuity of support from the hardware VP who left before we fully executed on our strategy, yet I can't think of any other workable choice given our constraints. Although I might be willing to repeat this strategy in the future if there were no other option, I strongly recommend trying to get buy-in for a broader change up front if at all possible.

Coaching Support

I was the only coach within the MCS division for the first year I was there. Although Trent and I traveled to India very early on, we didn't initially have sufficient coaching capacity to significantly influence things there. I delivered a few days of training and built relationships, but little else was practical.

In my second year, Trent managed to get enough funding to hire a few coaches in India. Finding better seasoned agile coaches in India is even harder than finding them in the US, yet after many months of interviewing I eventually found a few. After another month or so Trent and I managed to get the co-blessing of the India managers for these coaches and wrapped up the negotiations and on-boarding.

Waterfall Pressures on India-Based BIOS Engineers

As work related to the legacy Intel chipsets tapered off, several BIOS engineers based in India started contributing to the BIOS codebase for the new Intel chipset. The India engineers were kept fully aware of the common Definition of Done and related norms of the LeSS-oriented BIOS teams. Unfortunately, their management was still being driven in a waterfall fashion.

The early San Francisco members of the BIOS Scrum teams were adamant about not letting the quality they had worked so hard to improve be allowed to erode. The San Francisco BIOS team members improved their continuous integration practices, improved their integration test automation, performed frequent review of any code changes, and had lots of heart to heart conversations with the India BIOS engineers. These tactical solutions definitely made a positive impact and partially mitigated some of the issues.

Mitya and I had anticipated these problems. We had intentionally designed the BIOS component boundary so as to delay the organizational battle until greater political momentum favored winning. The intentional delay had ensured qualified agile coaches were available in the India office, the US based BIOS LeSS teams had jelled, and there was significant proof of massive improvements in quality and forecast transparency within the BIOS LeSS teams.

Mitya, Trent, and I recognized it was going to take a good bit of effort and shuttle diplomacy to resolve the underlying structural issues. We were ready to drive the structural issues to crises such that we could solve them. Unfortunately, the roughly concurrent loss of the supportive hardware VP and the massive layoffs crippled our strategy.

You can see the confluence of these various elements using a combination of the *Agile Adoption Timeline* diagram, *Organizational Structure* diagram sequence, and *BIOS Extended Component Team Expansion By MCS Hardware Generation* diagrams.

The Support System Collapses

Towards the end of my tenure in the Nakashima MCS division there were massive changes in the reporting structure, divisional funding, headcount, and senior management.

With eroding market share and a maturing competitive landscape, the MCS revenues were shrinking. There was a decision by the C suite of Nakashima to radically downsize the MCS division. The result was to reduce divisional headcount by about half. Many people at Nakashima told me it was the largest layoff they had ever seen at Nakashima. At least half of the BIOS teams would soon be laid off.

Prior to the layoffs many people in the management layer were being recruited to an exceptionally well funded start-up company. This included the VP to whom Mitya originally reported. Mitya then began reporting to the Software VP who had never been fully supportive of Scrum and agile to begin with. Not too long after my departure Mitya followed his prior VP to the new startup company.

Although I remained after the layoffs occurred it became politically untenable for Trent to renew my contract. The market rate and travel costs for an agile consultant are easily enough to pay for at least two or three engineers. Had it been up to Trent I would likely have had my contract extended, but even Trent had to obtain budgetary sign-off a couple layers up. A little over a year later Trent also left Nakashima.

Conclusion

Reflections on Deep Organizational Change

In retrospect the early loss of the supportive engineering SVP coupled with the lack of long-term job safety in a culture of frequent layoffs focused on short-term quick fixes of profit margins drastically reduced the odds of long-term success in transforming the organizational structure and culture. Without these challenges I believe success within the BIOS component could have been leveraged into a broader LeSS adoption.

After the success of the LeSS adoption within BIOS, I believe the original engineering SVP would have helped achieve the broader enrollment of senior management that was required to go further. Instead the senior management was busy scrambling to push out the upcoming MCS release while struggling to navigate the political landscape of an impending layoff. I believe more aggressive structural changes earlier on would have been very helpful, yet I don't think the senior management involved would have been ready to accept it without the time we took to slowly build up a record of success.

I am reminded of the parable of the sower in which a farmer casts seeds broadly over a variety of soil conditions. Although the seeds cast on shallow soil germinated and grew quickly, they soon withered under the sun for lack of deep roots. In contrast, seeds cast on deeper soil produced an abundant crop. Failure to properly prepare the soil for a LeSS adoption is likely to result in problems over the long-term, even though you will often encounter dramatic success early on. The soil for the BIOS LeSS adoption was sufficiently deep to produce some great early results, yet not quite deep enough to reach its abundant potential.

Summary of Benefits

The BIOS teams started as extended component teams while moving towards *expanded* component teams and feature teams. Benefits included:

- Locally improved **adaptability** and **value delivery** within the extended component boundary
    - Prior Observations:
        - Only one or two people understood a given BIOS sub-component. Code ownership and knowledge was effectively at the individual file level.
        - Knowledge of the codebase outside of the BIOS component was almost non-existent within the BIOS engineering group.
        - No one person was aware of the entirety of the work required to bring up a new Intel CPU generation on new blade hardware. Each BIOS firmware engineer and BIOS firmware tester only understood their small piece of the puzzle.
    - Prior Impacts:
        - BIOS engineers could not choose the most valuable work at any point in time, because they were restricted to their individual area of expertise.
        - It was nearly impossible to accurately forecast completion.
    - Subsequent Observations:
        - Every team member was slowly becoming comfortable working on a broader number of BIOS sub-components than they previously were.
        - Many BIOS team members were becoming increasingly skilled in testing and modifying every aspect of the overall system along the execution path between the GUI and the BIOS component.
        - Every BIOS team member had a good overall understanding of the work required to bring up a new Intel CPU. Any member of any of the LeSS-oriented BIOS teams could explain any item on the BIOS component backlog and how it fit into the overall picture.
        - The BIOS component backlog consistently provided an up to date view into all of the known remaining work required to ship the upcoming BIOS release.

- The BIOS teams accepted the natural variability of product development, and committed to *quality* (not *scope*) as explicitly expressed in the BIOS Definition of Done.

- Subsequent Impacts:

    - The LeSS-oriented BIOS teams were able to consistently focus on the most valuable work at any point in time.

    - The BIOS teams were far more confident in their release forecasts.

    - The BIOS teams were able to ensure a releasable level of functionality was achieved before working on lower priority functionality.

    - The LeSS-oriented BIOS extended component teams ensured every Sprint Increment was successfully integrated and tested with the MCS system as a whole. Across a few thousand engineers, only the small Diagnostics pilot Scrum team could claim anything similar.

- Improved technical practices that created **improved quality**, along with improved awareness of what additional improvements could bring

  - Prior Observations:

    - There was no common agreement on what the quality standards were.

    - Changes in the BIOS code supplied by AMI were co-mingled with the MCS specific code in a difficult to maintain fashion. Every new generation Intel CPU effectively required starting from scratch.

  - Prior Impacts:

    - Adapting MCS to each new generation of Intel CPU took over a year and an army of BIOS engineers. Failure to complete this work before Intel officially released a new CPU would result in tens of millions in lost revenue.

  - Subsequent Observations:

    - The BIOS Definition of Done is a living quality standard embraced by each of the new BIOS teams. The Definition of Done is continually clarified and extended over time by the teams themselves.

    - The BIOS Definition of Done has always included a commitment to ensure any MCS BIOS changes leverage the AMI plugin layer whenever possible. This sensible requirement originated within the teams, not from the coach or management.

- Subsequent Impacts:
    - Improved technical practices are expected to help dramatically reduce the time required to adapt to future generations of Intel CPUs.
    - Healthy retrospectives and a focus on quality continuously provide clarity on the next improvement.

- Early identification and resolution of **defects** related to the extended component
  - Prior Observations:
    - BIOS firmware engineers would make code changes and then throw the code over the wall to the testing group. It would generally be weeks or even months before the testers would identify problems and throw them back over the wall to the BIOS firmware engineers.
    - There was very little if any automated testing. Almost all testing was very manual.
    - It was common practice to commit code to source control which had compilation problems.
  - Prior Impacts:
    - It generally took months before defects were found and resolved.
    - BIOS engineers often wasted time chasing breaking changes introduced by another developer. Many times this was done by another developer in a distant time zone who was no longer at work when the problem was discovered.
  - Subsequent Observations:
    - Every BIOS team contained people with the skills and domain knowledge to both develop and test any changes.
    - Each BIOS team typically focused on making a small number of changes at any one time. They worked as real teams rather than as individuals as they actively focused on achieving the Definition of Done for the relevant Product Backlog Item.
    - BIOS team members actively cross-trained each other in both technical and domain knowledge. Testers became stronger developers, and developers became stronger testers.
    - Increasing levels of automated testing, and automated build systems helped further ensure problems were discovered as early as possible.

- The automated builds and tests were especially helpful in identifying conflicting priorities between the legacy teams and the LeSS-oriented teams.

- Subsequent Impacts:

  - Defects were found and resolved within minutes or hours rather than months. The usual months wasted in multiple months of bug squashing after a "code-freeze" were completely unnecessary.

  - Conflicting quality incentives and goals of the overseas teams working in the legacy structure became extremely visible once the overseas teams started to work on the same codebase. With time and management continuity I believe this visibility would have made it politically viable to restructure and improve the overseas teams as well.

- Improved employee **collaboration, engagement, and learning** within the extended component teams

  - Prior Observations:

    - People worked as individuals rather than team members, each person focused on their own personal assignments.

    - The teams followed a typical engagement model in which the manager led and drove the interactions and work assignments.

    - Growth and learning was limited to an individual's area of responsibility and historical expertise. Expanding one's expertise and responsibilities into new areas required arranging and shifting assignments. This took time, and was not always practical.

  - Prior Impacts:

    - *"A lot of effort with limited returns."* – Mitya

  - Subsequent Observations:

    - The teams managed the work themselves, collectively and enthusiastically focusing on delivering the PBIs their team selected.

    - Individuals and teams actively learned whatever was required to complete the PBI their team was focused on at the moment. The degree of knowledge transfer within and across teams was an order of magnitude greater than previously observed.

- Subsequent Impacts:

    - In the terminology of *Leading Teams* by Richard Hackman, BIOS teams acted as *real teams* rather than loosely collaborating individuals. Each team had a clear team *task*, clear *boundaries*, clearly specified *authority* to manage their own work processes, and membership *stability* over time.

- Increased awareness of **organizational impediments** and the need to make even more organizational changes

    - Prior Observations:

        - Long development cycles, late discovery of defects, frequent hand-offs cross teams, work becoming bottlenecked on a single individual, and lots of other problems were accepted as normal. There was very little awareness that things could be significantly better.

        - Individual team members had little structural incentive to focus on adaptability or value delivery at a global level.

        - There was very little discussion or effort taken to remove long-standing organizational impediments.

    - Prior Impacts:

        - There were very few productive efforts at improving adaptability and value delivery at a global level.

    - Subsequent Observations:

        - Regular team and overall retrospectives within the BIOS teams frequently identified organizational impediments, which the teams and management would then actively attempt to resolve.

        - The efforts of the BIOS extended component teams to fully validate any BIOS changes increasingly drove them to challenge code ownership boundaries and expand their ability to make code changes across multiple components.

        - The pursuit of more rigorous quality standards manifested in the BIOS Definition of Done helped highlight the conflicting structural incentives of the legacy BIOS teams.

    - Subsequent Impacts:

        - People were slowly waking up to what was possible, and the need for greater organizational change.

Wrapping Up

I strongly believe the best chance of long-term success is achieved with a broad product boundary coupled with feature teams executing within the full scope of the product. If the art of the possible excludes this choice, an incremental approach starting with extended component teams and aggressively moving towards expanded component teams and feature teams can still be worth pursuing.

Appreciations

I am grateful for the extensive work and mentorship provided by Viktor Grgic and Craig Larman throughout the editorial review process.

Contact Information

Thank you for taking the time to read the case study. Please feel free to reach out with any questions or thoughts you may have. I welcome an opportunity to be a part of your journey in improving your own organization.

James Carpenter

Certified LeSS Trainer

Cell: +1 832-677-724

Email: james@agilecarpentry.com

Website: https://agilecarpentry.com

LinkedIn: https://www.linkedin.com/in/jamescarpenter1/

www.ingramcontent.com/pod-product-compliance
Lightning Source LLC
LaVergne TN
LVHW070901210926
848482LV00016B/991